Solid Ground

Solid Ground

The Inerrant Word of God in an Errant World

EDITED BY

GABRIEL N. E. FLUHRER

PUBLISHING
P.O. BOX 817 • PHILLIPSBURG • NEW JERSEY 08865-0817

Unless otherwise indicated, Scripture quotations are from *ESV Bible®* (*The Holy Bible, English Standard Version®*). Copyright © 2001 by Crossway Bibles, a publishing ministry of Good News Publishers. Used by permission. All rights reserved.

Scripture quotation marked (NASB) is from the *NEW AMERICAN STAN-DARD BIBLE®*. © Copyright The Lockman Foundation 1960, 1962, 1963, 1968, 1971, 1972, 1973, 1975, 1977. Used by permission.

Italics within Scripture quotations indicate emphasis added.

Printed in the United States of America

Library of Congress Cataloging-in-Publication Data

Philadelphia Conference on Reformed Theology.
  Solid ground : the inerrant word of God in an errant world / edited by Gabriel N.E. Fluhrer.
     p. cm.
  Proceedings of conferences held 1975-2007.
  Includes bibliographical references.
  ISBN 978-1-59638-403-3 (pbk.)
  1. Bible--Evidences, authority, etc.--Congresses. 2. Reformed Church--Doctrines--Congresses. I. Fluhrer, Gabriel N. E., 1978- II. Title.
  BS480.P46 2012
  220.1--dc23
                                        2011047685

To Dr. James Montgomery Boice,

Whose vision, leadership, passion, and unfailing trust in the
inerrant Word of God
was the foundation for the Philadelphia Conference on
Reformed Theology,

who blessed and continues to bless so many lives with that
same vision:

"And I heard a voice from heaven saying,
'Write this: Blessed are the dead who die in the Lord from
now on.'
'Blessed indeed,' says the Spirit, 'that they may rest from their
labors, for their deeds follow them!' "
Rev. 14:13

Contents

Editor's Preface   ix

1. On Knowing God: The World and the Word   1
   J. I. PACKER

2. The Sufficient Word of God   19
   J. LIGON DUNCAN III

3. The Truth of God   39
   R. C. SPROUL

4. Scripture Alone   51
   JAMES M. BOICE

5. God's Mighty Word   73
   RICHARD D. PHILLIPS

6. The Word in the Church   85
   MARK DEVER

7. The Accessible Word   105
   PHILIP GRAHAM RYKEN

8. Preaching: The Means of Revival   131
   EDMUND P. CLOWNEY

Editor's Preface

How firm a foundation, ye saints of the Lord,
is laid for your faith in his excellent Word!
What more can he say than to you he hath said,
you who unto Jesus for refuge have fled?[1]

THIS IS A BOOK about the Book, the Word of God written. Over the past decade or so, some within evangelicalism have begun to question whether Scripture is worthy of the definite article. That is, some have suggested that we ought to treat the Bible as *a* book—even a very special book—but not *the* Book that perfectly illumines all things. The Bible's unique features and religious value, it is subtly suggested, owe more to the powerful way in which God uses it in our lives than to a divine authority inherent in the text itself. The dangers that lurk behind these and other attempts to reinterpret or otherwise diminish the Bible's claim to be God-breathed (2 Tim. 3:16) are not unimagined. They not only chip away at the full confidence that believers

1. "How Firm a Foundation," in John Rippon, *A Selection of Hymns* (1787), hymn K.

must have in the trustworthiness of Scripture, but also rob its Author of the full glory that his Word displays and demands.

The essays featured in this book explore that glory—the glory of the triune God—by unfolding the richness and perfections of the Bible. They were originally addresses delivered at the Philadelphia Conference on Reformed Theology (PCRT) from 1975 to 2007 by pastors and theologians who find their life and breath in the pages of Scripture. The addresses have been edited for ease of reading but retain much, if not most, of their original wording.

Each generation must own for itself the cardinal truths of the faith once for all delivered to the saints, and ours is no exception. Indeed, in my own estimation, our generation is in danger of seeing what is perhaps *the* most central doctrine of the Christian faith—the doctrine of the inspired and concomitant inerrancy of Scripture—eclipsed to a degree previously unknown in the modern era.

This assertion may sound overstated, if not alarmist, but the Enlightenment's attempt to enshrine human autonomy in every area of life is now bearing its bitter fruit in how Christians think about their Bibles. To be sure, we are not at all surprised when the world, lost and dead in sins and trespasses, scoffs at the Word of God. But we must be surprised and heartbroken when the same sounds of protest against the truth of God's Word come to us in siren song from those who claim the name of Christ—indeed, by those who claim to be evangelicals.

For this reason, the Alliance of Confessing Evangelicals is proud to present the current volume. Its authors aim to be accessible, pastoral, and clear, much like the Bible they revere. They do not revel in polemics, though polemics are inevitable in "this present evil age" (Gal. 1:4 NASB) and so are presented by some of the authors. Their supreme desire, however, is to issue a clarion call for the church to return to its central, long-standing, and vital conviction that the Bible is the Word of God, and so without error in its original autographs, the only infallible rule of faith and practice.

Chapter 1 opens with J. I. Packer unfolding the well-nigh unspeakable privilege that Christians enjoy as those who can know God through his Word. Next, J. Ligon Duncan III brings his experience as a seasoned pastor to explain why the Scriptures are sufficient for us to know God and live in a manner pleasing to him. In chapter 3, R. C. Sproul, as only Sproul can, blends anecdotes from his own storied career with hard-hitting application on why the Bible is true.

Our fourth essay is from the pen of Dr. James Montgomery Boice, the late chair and founder of the PCRT. He offers a helpful pastoral overview of the meaning of *sola Scriptura*, the rallying cry of the Protestant Reformation's commitment to the Bible. Then in chapter 5, current PCRT chairman Richard D. Phillips masterfully unfolds the fifty-fifth chapter of Isaiah—a vital passage in formulating a sound doctrine of Scripture. Chapter 6 finds Mark Dever laying out a case for the centrality of the Word for the church. And in chapter 7, Philip Ryken gives the reader a scholarly and unapologetic case for the clarity of God's Word. Given the current fog of postmodern denials of the clarity of language, Dr. Ryken's treatment here is particularly timely.

Finally, as with the first volume of historical PCRT addresses,[2] this book closes with an essay on the implications of the churchly doctrine of Scripture for preaching. With his trademark passion and exegetical sensitivity, Dr. Edmund Clowney pleads with those of us who stand behind the sacred desk week by week to

2. Gabriel N. E. Fluhrer, ed., *Atonement* (Phillipsburg, NJ: P&R Publishing, 2010).

be held captive to the Word of God, for it is the primary means for true revival in the church today.

As with any book project, there are as always more people to thank than space for writing. Here I simply extend my heartfelt gratitude to Bob Brady, executive vice president of the Alliance, and the entire staff of the Alliance for their tireless efforts in service of a modern reformation while exhibiting a contagiously cheerful disposition. In particular, Bob's leadership at the Alliance has made our work a true joy. I would also like to thank the volunteers and donors of the Alliance who make our work possible.

I would like to thank Marvin Padgett and all the editors and staff at P&R Publishing for their patience, support, and partnership in the publishing of these Alliance volumes. Their commitment to see the truths expounded at the PCRT brought to a wider audience is a gift of God's grace.

My profound thanks and deep appreciation also go to the Rev. Richard D. Phillips, the chair of the PCRT and, in so many ways, the successor to Dr. Boice's vision. Rev. Phillips is a dear friend and mentor, as well as a champion of the truths contained in this book. May his tribe increase!

In addition to the stalwarts represented in this volume, I must also recognize the professors under whom I've had the privilege of studying. To Drs. Scott Oliphint, Lane Tipton, Jeffrey Jue, David Garner, Richard Gaffin, Carl Trueman, Vern Poythress, William Edgar, Joseph Pipa, Benjamin Shaw, John Carrick, Tony Curto, Sidney Dyer, C. N. Willborn, James McGoldrick, and others: please accept my sincere thanks for your commitment and labors for the defense of the truth of the Word of God to the good of my own life and the life of the church.

Finally, to my dear wife and little girls, I would not know how to minister the precious Word without your love and support. Daily I marvel at God's grace for giving me such a competent, caring, and godly wife, as well as children who love to hear God's Word.

It goes without saying that the Book, the Word of God written, directs our attention to the One who is the living Word of God—Jesus Christ. I remain firmly convinced that only the stoutest doctrine of inspiration—the doctrine our Lord himself taught (see John 10:35)—is the sole hope for both the world and the church, for it assures us that the gospel we preach is not in vain. Without an errorless Bible, we cannot truly know the gospel, and without the gospel, we cannot know the Word incarnate and so would remain without hope, without God, in the world. But thanks be to God for the Bible and for the Christ of whom it flawlessly speaks!

The remarks of Cornelius Van Til, the celebrated Westminster apologist (and defender of the church's doctrine of inspiration), form a fitting conclusion to this overlong introduction.[3] In his introduction to B. B. Warfield's seminal work on the doctrine of Scripture, *The Inspiration and Authority of the Bible*, Dr. Van Til wrote:

> Only in a return to the Bible as infallibly inspired in its autography is there hope for science, for philosophy and for theology. Without returning to this Bible, science and philosophy may flourish with borrowed capital as the prodigal flourished for a while with his father's substance. But the prodigal had no self-sustaining principle. No man has till he accepts the Scripture that Warfield presents.[4]

Gabriel N. E. Fluhrer

3. I am indebted to the Rev. R. Carlton Wynne for his many helpful comments on this preface.

4. Cornelius Van Til, "Introduction," in B. B. Warfield, *The Inspiration and Authority of the Bible* (Philadelphia: Presbyterian and Reformed, 1948), 68.

1

On Knowing God: The World and the Word

J. I. PACKER

But now . . . you have come to know God,
or rather to be known by God. (Gal. 4:9)

ONE OF THE MOST AMAZING claims that the Bible makes is found in the first half of Galatians 4:9: "But now that you have come to know God, or rather to be known by God, how can you turn back again to the weak and worthless elementary principles of the world, whose slaves you want to be once more?" Paul makes a claim here, and he makes it on behalf of all the Christians in the Galatian churches. He says, "You have come to know God, or rather to be known by God." Now, that claim can be made on behalf of every true Christian in every age and in every place. And what a tremendous thing that is to be able to say! To know God is the promise of the gospel. To know God is the supreme gift of God's grace.

A Scriptural Promise

This, of course, was the burden and the quintessence of Jeremiah's prophecy of the new covenant (Jer. 31:31–34). What would happen when the new covenant came? Why, all people included in that gracious covenant would *know God*. Recall the prophet's words: "For they shall all know me, from the least of them to the greatest, declares the LORD" (v. 34).

We see the same idea when we witness our Lord praying to his Father in John 17:3: "And this is eternal life, that they know you the only true God, and Jesus Christ whom you have sent." And the claim is echoed by John in his first letter: "And we know that the Son of God has come and has given us understanding, so that we may know him who is true; and we are in him who is true, in his Son Jesus Christ. He is the true God and eternal life" (1 John 5:20).

God is telling us that we can know him. We can know him—the One who is real. The One who will deliver us from illusion to know the One who, in truth, is a strong tower and a real rock to those who trust in him. Yes, this is what we were made for, and this is what we were redeemed for.

We might take the thought further and say that the perfection of the knowledge of God and of his Son Jesus Christ is the sum of the real Christian's ambition and hope. Paul declares just such an ambition, first in Philippians 3:10: "that I may know him and the power of his resurrection, and may share his sufferings, becoming like him in his death"; and again in

1 Corinthians 13:12: "For now we see in a mirror dimly, but then face to face. Now I know in part; then I shall know fully, even as I have been fully known." Yes, it is man's highest dignity and it is man's final fulfillment to know his God and the Son of God, perfectly.

I wonder, do you believe this? Or is what I have been writing mere words on a page? Knowing God is the great theme—indeed, the central and glorious theme—of the Scriptures. Think of it! Through Christ man knows God, or rather is known by God.

Calvin's "Great Theme"

I remember hearing Dr. R. C. Sproul once say, "Knowledge of God is a key theme in Reformed theology." This is one of the secrets of its strength. And the first (and in many ways the best) expositor of this great theme is the man who stands as the fountainhead of Reformed theology—that towering man, that great genius—John Calvin. Lest I leave you with the wrong idea of Calvin by speaking of him in those terms, let me add that he was a humble man who, by faith, knew God and was known by God, as you and I may be.

Calvin wrote the classic textbook of Reformed Christianity, the *Institutes of the Christian Religion*. I commend this magnum opus of Calvin to you; it takes a lot to get through it, but it is very much worth it! The *Institutes* went through five editions. And one of the things that one traces as one follows it through the successive editions of the book is the way in which this theme of knowing God expanded as Calvin developed the book. In the first edition (ca. 1536), his only real reference (at least his only explicit reference) to the theme of knowing God

3

was in the first sentence, in which he declared that the sum of sacred doctrine is just about contained in these two parts: the knowledge of God and of ourselves.[1] From the second edition onward, however, not only did the book open with that same sentence (with one minor change: Calvin substituted the word *wisdom* for *knowledge*), but Calvin gave a full chapter to each of these themes.

When he finally came to cast the *Institutes* into its ultimate form—the fifth edition of 1559, twenty-three years after the first edition—not only did he leave those first two chapters of the first book as they had been since the second edition, but in turn, he actually devoted the *entire first book* of the work to the knowledge of God the Creator and the entire second book to the knowledge of Christ the Redeemer! Thus, the theme of the knowledge of God becomes the overarching theme of the whole of the *Institutes* and the entire concern of the first two books. Incidentally, the third book goes on to the knowledge of the grace of Christ and how to obtain and enjoy it.

Note as well that Calvin's book was not called the *Institutes of Christian Theology* but the *Institutes of the Christian Religion*. This is really to make the point again that we made above: for Reformed folk there is no gap, no gulf, no change of gears between theology and religion. *Religion* means "godliness." True theology, as Reformed people understand it, leads straight into godliness; that is what it is for. And Calvin knew that very clearly. That's why he called his book *Institutes of the Christian Religion*. And that's why he expounds the knowledge of God and the knowledge of Christ and the knowledge of grace in a practical way as he does.

1. John Calvin, *Institutes of the Christian Religion*, ed. John T. McNeill, trans. Ford Lewis Battles, Library of Christian Classics (London: SCM, 1960), 35.

Thus, knowing God, for Calvin, meant not the cultivating of theological skill, but the practice of Christian obedience, the practice of Christian religion in the best sense of the term. So in studying this subject of knowing God, we are on to the central and very much practical theme of Christianity, as Calvin and his followers understood it. That is our goal in our study: living out what we know of God and his ways.

What It Means to Know God

What does it mean to speak of knowing God? Let us take the concept, put it under the microscope, and try to analyze it. And in order to get our minds quite clear on this, let me begin by stating four things to prepare the way for the final thing I want to state in addition to these first four.

Knowing God Is More than an Awareness of God

First, knowing God—and let us be clear about this—is more than the natural man's awareness of God. Now, there is such a thing. If men say that they do not acknowledge God, that does not mean that no inklings of God have ever gotten through to them. Rather, it means that the notions of God that have gotten through to them have been denied by them. So says Paul in the first chapter of Romans; and so says Calvin, who had studied that chapter and listened to what it said.

Calvin has a number of phrases to express this inescapable awareness that the natural man has of the Creator whom he ought to serve and who will call him to account one day. Calvin talks of the *sensus divinitatus*, the "sense of deity." What is the *sensus divinitatus*? It is a sort of persuasion, the persuasion that there is a God. Calvin also called it the "seed of religion," the "inclination to religion," and the "notion of God." These are all phrases that he used to express this inescapable awareness that there is a God whom men ought to worship.

To be sure, Calvin doesn't call this knowledge of God by the same Latin word that he uses for the Christian's knowledge of God. He calls it *notitia*, or, we might say, *awareness*. And the word that he reserves for the Christian knowledge of God is *cognitia*, or *knowledge* in the whole sense. Nonetheless, he insists that the natural man's awareness of God is something inescapable. Paraphrasing Calvin, then: "Though he tries to escape it, he cannot." This is precisely what Paul is saying in Romans 1:18–23.

The knowledge of God that the natural man possesses is covenantal knowledge. It is knowledge that involves a personal commitment on both sides. It is knowledge of the covenant God who men know is their God. To paraphrase Martin Luther, religion is a matter of personal pronouns. This means that religion, the Christian religion, is a matter of being able to say, "my God," "my Lord," "my Savior," and of knowing that God says of you, "my child," "my person."

Thus, knowledge of God exists in that relationship—and apart from that relationship, there is something less than true and full knowledge of God. Knowledge of God, in the sense of *cognitia*, is more than mere awareness that there is a God. Knowledge of God includes and involves communion with God. It is found only in a covenant relationship in which God is your God and you are his person.

Knowing God Is More than Any Particular Experience

In the second place, knowledge of God is more than any particular experience of God. Now, this may sound shocking to you, but it is true. Let Calvin teach us. Calvin, like the Bible, came from an era when people were less self-absorbed than we tend to be today. In Calvin's day, people tended to be more concerned about the realities that they experienced than the experiences themselves. We, unhappily, live in an age that is "experience-conscious" and "experience-centered." So we generally jump to the conclusion that the more intense any experience is, the more of God there must be in it.

Now, that isn't so. There are many intense experiences in life, but it would be very foolish to suppose that just because they are intense, they are therefore full of God. And it's even more foolish when people today take drugs and expose themselves to other artificial stimuli in order to intensify their own experiences, believing that in any intense experience God is present. That's not the way it comes. Knowledge of God isn't even to be identified with a conversion experience, although without knowledge of God in the sense in which we're speaking of it, no conversion experience would ever be. But what I want to say here is this: knowing God is something far bigger, far richer, and embracing far more than any particular experience. Within the knowledge of God, experiences come—yes, praise God, they do!—in all kinds of ways: conversion experiences and other experiences in the Christian life.

Knowing God, however, is a matter of the relationship itself. It is being aware of that relationship. Of cultivating that relationship. Of counting on that relationship. Of knowing that that relationship stands even when you've got a headache and a toothache and you feel rotten and your experience is simply one of depression and gloom. Knowing God is more, I say, than any particular experience of God. Do let us get that clear. It is the biggest thing in life to get this second point clear, especially in this day and age: knowing God is more than simply an intense experience.

Knowing God Is More than Simply Knowing about God

And then, third: knowing God, according to Scripture, according to Calvin, is more than merely knowing *about* God. Although knowledge about God is basic to knowing him, there is something more. Calvin, in fact, was quite clear on what needs to be known about God. In the very first edition of the *Institutes*, he specified four things that need to be known about God. Listen to him:

> First, he is infinite wisdom, righteousness, goodness, mercy, truth, power and life, so that there is no other wisdom, righteousness, goodness, mercy, truth, power and life save in him. And wherever we perceive any of these things they are of him. And the second thing we must know is that all things both in heaven and earth were created to his glory. And the third thing we must know is that he is a righteous judge, sternly punishing those that swerve from his laws and do not entirely perform his will. And fourth, he is mercy and gentleness, receiving kindly the wretched and poor that flee to his clemency and trust themselves to his faithfulness.[2]

That's the knowledge of God. He's the One in whom all value abides. He is the Creator of all things. He is the Judge of all men, and he is the Giver of all grace. "These are the four things we must know about God," says Calvin. Let all believers add their hearty *Amen* to such sentiments!

But Calvin was the first to insist that there is more to knowing God than simply mastering this description of God and thus knowing about him. All the Reformers were concerned to teach and develop all these four heads of truth about God that Calvin has mentioned. But all the Reformers, with Calvin, were also

2. Calvin, *Institutes*, 1.10.2.

concerned to insist that, however right our structured knowledge of God may be—and the Reformers wanted to see us clear on our knowledge about God—nonetheless, personal knowledge of God goes beyond all that. The knowledge that they sought, and the knowledge to which they directed us, and the knowledge to which Paul directs us, is what modern philosophers would call not knowledge by description only, but knowledge by acquaintance, too.[3]

Let me illustrate what I mean by this distinction. I can know a great deal about the British Prime Minister, or the American President, but I don't know either of them. I have knowledge by description concerning both, yet I have knowledge by acquaintance in regard to neither. But I have knowledge by acquaintance in relation, say, to my friends and family, whom I know and rejoice to know. You see the difference. And knowledge of God, say the Scriptures, is more than merely knowledge *about* God.

Knowing God, Knowing Ourselves

The fourth and final negative I put in a deliberately paradoxical way: knowing God is more than knowing God. You say, "What do you mean?" I mean this: you cannot know God without coming to know yourself, too. And if you decline to know yourself, as the Scriptures introduce you to yourself, well, then you can never know God as the Scriptures present him.

For how does the Bible introduce us to "us"? By telling us that whereas we thought we were doing pretty well and were pretty fine people on the whole, we are, in truth, poor and blind and naked and wretched in God's sight. We are sinners, and we've been ruined by our sin. Reformed theology has always stressed

3. Bertrand Russell, *Mysticism and Logic and Other Essays* (London: George Allen & Unwin, 1917), 209–10.

this more perhaps than any other expression of Christianity that the world has ever seen. And it has stressed it both for the sake of being realistic about ourselves and for the sake of true knowledge of God.

You say, "What's the connection between this and the true knowledge of God?" Why, the connection is just this: God is the One who comes right down to us in our desperate need, and in his Son, Jesus Christ, brings us the mercy and the grace and the help and the new life that we need in order to raise us up again. And the more clearly we understand ourselves and our sin, then the more richly we are able to understand the glory of God's grace. How right was Calvin when he said that the sum of our wisdom is comprehended in the knowledge of God and of ourselves.[4] And Calvin went on to say, "The two go together." That is the point I'm trying to make.

So knowing God is more than knowing God. There's a sense in which God is incomprehensible to us, "in his essence," as Calvin used to say. In the mystery of the life of the Father, Son, and Spirit, eternally blessed in their fellowship together, God is incomprehensible. In the mystery of all his deep thoughts and of all his plans for world history, he is just beyond our grasp; in that sense, he is incomprehensible to us. He is too "big," as it were, for us to wrap our minds around.

But, to paraphrase Calvin again, in the knowledge of God that the Scriptures talk about, the point is not that our minds have comprehended the great and, indeed, incomprehensible deity. Rather, the point is that we as sinners who know ourselves and our need have come to know the God who is infinitely gracious. We have come to know him whose mercy avails to meet all our needs and to make our ruined humanity new again.

4. Calvin, *Institutes*, 1.1.1.

That's what the knowing of God is all about; it is knowing God in Christ as a Savior.

The Knowledge of God: Apprehension, Application, Adoration

Positively stated, then, let me say this. You ask what the knowledge of God is, as Reformed people understand it, as the Scriptures present it. Well, I'll give you a formula for it. *Knowledge of God is apprehension plus application plus adoration.* It is apprehending God as he discloses himself in the gospel of Christ. It is applying the promise of the gospel to our lives. And it is adoring the God who has thus come to us and become our God and our Savior. Let Calvin put it in his way: "The knowledge of God, as I understand it, is that by which we not only conceive that there is a God, but also grasp what benefits us and makes for his glory; what, in short, brings profit."[5] Calvin means, then, that in knowing God, we grasp his grace. "Nor shall we say, but God strictly speaking is known, where there is no religion or godliness," he says again.[6] There it is: apprehension, application, and adoration. There's religion or godliness. Or again, Calvin says, "We are called to a knowledge of God, which doesn't just flit about in the brain content with empty speculation, but which, if we rightly grasp it and it takes root in our hearts, will be solid and fruitful."[7] And again, another quote: "Knowledge of God is not identified with cold speculation, but it brings with it worship of him."[8]

5. Calvin, *Institutes*, 1.2.1.
6. Ibid.
7. Calvin, *Institutes*, 1.5.9.
8. Calvin, *Institutes*, 1.10.2.

The total notion of knowing God, which emerges in Calvin's *Institutes*, includes all this: acknowledging God as he reveals himself in Scripture; giving him honor and thanks for all things; humbling oneself before him as a needy sinner and learning of him as he speaks of salvation; believing on the Christ whom he sets forth as our Savior; then loving the Father and the Son with a love that answers the love that they have shown to us; living by faith in the promises of mercy that are given us in Christ; cherishing the hope of resurrection; obeying God's law; and seeking his glory in all relationships and all commerce with created things. So, you see, knowledge of God thus embraces both true theology and true religion: apprehension, application, adoration of God as he comes to us in Christ.

Knowing God through the Bible

But how is God to be known? What are the means of knowing God? Now, the usual Reformed answer to that question has been to say that the knowledge of God depends on God's revelation of himself. Yet I believe that the thrust of this confession will be clearer and more vivid to our minds if, in place of *revelation*, we substitute (just for a moment) the word *communication*.

Why do I suggest this substitution? It seems to me that the word *revelation* might suggest no more than the general display of something that is there to be inspected, if you like. When a monument is unveiled, the statue is revealed and then you can go and admire it. You don't have to, but it's there for you to go and inspect if you want to. I believe that the word *revelation* doesn't always signify to people's minds more than this; it is not as good a word as the word *communication* for conveying what, as scriptural Christians, we should be concerned to say about the way that knowledge of God comes. That word *communication*, it seems to me, has all the right vibrations. It conveys the thoughts of someone, in this case God approaching us, telling us something, presenting himself to us, asking us for our attention, actually giving us something. The word *communicate* naturally suggests all that.

And that is what God does. Remember, as Scripture reveals the human situation, it is showing us that man—and that means us—is made for loving fellowship with God. Actually, man apart from God is in a state of having turned his back on God, having turned away from God through sin, being set character-wise in the shape of the first sin that Adam and Eve committed in the garden. And what does man do in sin? Why, he does what Adam and Eve did. He plays God. He behaves as if he were the center of the universe and everything were there for him. Adam and Eve yielded to the temptation to be wise and to know good and evil without reference to God. They didn't want to depend on God anymore; that was the heart of their original sin: man plays God, and in playing God he has to fight God. He has to defy God. He has to deny God's claim on him. He has to say to God, "No, I'll not do what you say. I want to do what I think." And that's been the analysis and nature of sin ever since the garden of Eden.

Well, men and women—all of us—are under the power of sin by nature, alienated from God because of this wretched power. Our backs are turned to God, meaning there is no communication. If someone turns his back to you, that isn't a communication posture, is it? If you have your back turned to someone, it means that you don't want to talk to that person. But that's exactly what man is like in sin: man has his back turned to God. But God the Creator, in his mercy, does not give up on us. He still wants to have sinful men in fellowship with himself, so though man has ceased to communicate with God, God still communicates with man.

Three Stages of Communication

There is, as I said at the beginning, this general communication of God, this inescapable awareness of God, which comes to all men simply by virtue of being alive in God's world. Men reject it. They claim they don't know God simply because they've suppressed what they do know of God. So general revelation, the heavens declaring the glory of God, the firmament showing his handiwork, the invisible things of the Creator being known from the things that are made, that communication from God to men, produces no results. Men don't respond.

So God does more. What does he do? He gives us special communication. We call it *special revelation*. In this special communication from God, there are three stages. Stage 1 we will call *redemption in history*. By words and works, God makes himself known on the stage of history as the Savior of man. There was a typical salvation of Israel from Egypt. And then there was the great antitype, the final spiritual salvation, the glorious salvation wrought by Jesus Christ. God teaches us here about redemption in history, about redemption for a lost world.

And then comes stage 2 in the process of divine communication, which we will call *records and writing*. God inspires what Calvin called public records of the things that he'd done in history so that all men in every age might know what God had done and so come to benefit from what God had done. And we have those records in the Scriptures. The Bible is God's own interpretive account of what he has done

14

in history for man's salvation and how it applies to life and how it applies to us.

And then finally comes the third stage in God's process of communication, which we will call *reception by individuals*. Here we are concerned with the work of God the Spirit, taking the Word, opening it to us, and taking us and opening our hearts so that the Word finds entrance. This twofold opening—the opening of the Word and the opening of our hearts so that the Word comes in and we understand it—is what is covered by the New Testament use of the word *reveal*.

Take, for instance, what Jesus said of Simon Peter's confession of Caesarea of Philippi: "Blessed are you, Simon Bar-Jonah! For flesh and blood has not revealed this to you, but my Father who is in heaven" (Matt. 16:17). The word *reveal* is used the same way in Galatians 1:15–16: "But . . . he who had set me apart before I was born, and who called me by his grace, was pleased to reveal his Son to me."

Now, this is a pregnant verse for Paul. Surely the first thing it means is that on the Damascus road, Paul gained a very specific kind of knowledge about our Lord: the knowledge of who Jesus was, Son of God and Savior, just as the martyr Stephen had said in Paul's presence (see Acts 7:51–8:1). Indeed, Paul had thought it was quite right to stone Stephen, and had actually held the coats of the perpetrators while they stoned him and killed him. But knowledge of that same Jesus now came right into Paul's heart so that he knew it was all true and he couldn't deny it anymore. And God revealed his Son to Paul. Paul understood, and the Word came right in because God opened his heart to let it in.

And thus the Word is received by individuals. God, who commanded the light to shine out of darkness, shines in men's hearts to give the light of the knowledge of his glory in the face of Jesus Christ (see 2 Cor. 4:6). And thus, with Paul, we come to see that Jesus Christ is precisely the person that the New Testament says he is, the Son of God and the Savior of the world. And as we come to know who he is and as we come to respond to him and to all that he is, we know God.

The Centrality of the Bible
for the Knowledge of God

Now, in all of this the Bible is crucial; surely you can see that from the way that I put it. For if there were no oracles of God (Paul's phrase for the Scriptures—see Rom. 3:2) to set before us what God has done for the world—for us—on the stage of history, in space and time, through the death and resurrection of Jesus Christ, then we should never know—we could never know—God and his Christ. So the Bible is crucial, and Calvin in the first book of the *Institutes* underlines this point. He likens the Bible to spectacles, reasoning that we need such an apparatus because we are so shortsighted and have such a vague, fuzzy awareness of God. But when the Scriptures come to us, like spectacles, they clear up what is vague and fuzzy and tell us precisely who God is and what he has done for us. And then we're confronted with the real God, and the knowledge of God becomes a real possibility. It is no longer a fuzzy smudge, but it's something definite, something clear, something that calls us and challenges us.

And Calvin has another image: the image of the schoolmaster. Calvin talks about our ignorance, but Scripture comes to us as our schoolmaster, to be (paraphrasing Calvin here) the rule of our thinking and speaking of God. It comes to us to teach us what we are to think about him and his grace to sinners. It teaches us how we are to speak of him and how we are to trust him. We are clueless; we need instruction. The Scriptures are given to us to be our schoolmaster for this very reason. We are in a maze; that's a further image that Calvin uses. We are lost in a labyrinth; we just can't find our way out. That's Calvin's picture of sinners wandering lost and aimlessly and helplessly in this dark world. But, says Calvin, the Scriptures guide us out of the maze.

Yes, through the Scriptures, men may know God. Without the Scriptures, men could not know God, so says Calvin; the Scriptures are vital, and surely he's right. The formative, controlling, and crucial principle of Reformed theology is *sola Scriptura*: by Scripture alone is God known. And in Reformed theology, the Bible is thought of as God preaching, God teaching, God speaking—saying in application to us what he said long ago to his people when the Bible was first inspired, and through the same Word giving to us himself and his Son.

Thus, Reformed people turn their backs on speculative theology and they give their minds up to learn from the Scriptures. They thank God for the Scriptures. Not primarily, and ideally not at all, do they use the Scriptures simply as a club for beating other people over the head. To be sure, they do indeed use the Scriptures as a test for checking whether what men say in God's name is true; but first and foremost, Reformed people use the Scriptures as their own guide to life. They thank God for the Scriptures as the supreme and final glorious revelation that God has given. They know no Christ but the Christ of the Scriptures. They have no hope but in the promises of God in the Scriptures.

In closing, let me ask you: is the Bible to you, first and foremost, a gift of God's grace, the light for your feet and the lamp for your path in the darkness in which you are by nature? Let us learn from John Wesley, who was much more of a Calvinist than he knew. Wesley in the preface to his sermons wrote this:

17

I am a creature of a day, passing thro' life, as an arrow thro' the air . . . till a few moments hence, I am no more seen; I drop into an unchangeable eternity! I want to know one thing, the way to heaven. . . . God himself has condescended to teach the way. . . . He hath written it down in a book. O give me that book! At any price give me the book of God! I have it: Here is knowledge enough for me. . . . I sit down alone: Only God is here. In his presence I open, I read his book. . . . I lift up my heart to the Father of Lights. . . . And what I thus learn, that I teach.[9]

Yes, first and foremost, to a Reformed Christian (which is just a biblical Christian, I think) the Bible will be seen as a supreme gift of grace, the written Word given to us in our darkness, to light the way to the feet of the living Word, Jesus Christ, the Lord. Learn to love your Bibles, Christian friends, not simply as repositories of true propositions, but as the path to the Savior's feet. That is the Reformed way. That is the way to the true knowledge of our God, to whom be praise and glory forever.

9. John Wesley, *Sermons on Several Occasions* (Leeds: Edward Baines, 1799), vi.

2

The Sufficient
Word of God

J. LIGON DUNCAN III

*All Scripture is breathed out by God and profitable
for teaching, for reproof, for correction, and for
training in righteousness. (2 Tim. 3:16)*

IS THE WORD OF GOD sufficient for our needs as
believers? Paul gives us an answer to that question in the third
chapter of his second letter to Timothy. I want to draw your
attention to verse 12 of that chapter as we begin: "Indeed, all who
desire to live a godly life in Christ Jesus will be persecuted." The
context of this passage, then, is the apostle Paul giving instruc-
tions to Timothy and to the Christians at Ephesus about living
a godly life. Specifically, he is instructing them about living a
godly life in the midst of persecution.

Now, our examination of verses 14–17 will be fairly straightforward. Paul essentially says two things to Timothy. First, he tells him to live by the Book. And the second thing he says is this: "Live by the Book, Timothy, because its words come right out of God's mouth." God's Book, then, is the most practical book in the world, for it tells you how to live with God.

Remember, though, that Paul is writing to a young pastor who is a son in the faith, a son in the Lord to him. The apostle Paul expects these words to be read aloud to the congregation. We understand that by simply looking at the content of what the apostle says here in chapter 3. It is interesting to note in this passage that Paul gives instruction for the qualifications for elders, among other things. Now, Timothy was already an elder or overseer, which is what the original word means. He didn't necessarily need to know the qualifications for an elder, but the congregation needed to know. It was going to be their obligation to identify appropriate, gifted, and called men who had the qualifications listed in Paul's letter. And so the apostle Paul expects this letter to be read aloud to the congregation and the congregation to be edified by it.

So not only is Paul telling Timothy that he is to live and minister by the Book, he's telling the whole congregation that they are to live and minister by the Book. This was and is, of course, because the Bible is ultimately not just Paul's word; it is God's Word. And in this very passage he tells us that he wrote these words for our edification so that *we* would live by the Book.

The Protestant Reformers and the Sufficiency of Scripture

Our topic in this chapter is the sufficiency of Scripture. What do we mean when we speak of the sufficiency of Scripture? We mean that the Bible, God's infallible Word, is fully adequate and authoritative for salvation and sanctification, for evangelism and edification, for faith and for life. And some of our great Reformation creeds give us good, brief descriptions of just what we are affirming when we speak of the doctrine of the sufficiency of Scripture.

For instance, the Westminster Confession of Faith, which is a creed written in London during the middle part of the seventeenth century, gives a clear statement about the sufficiency of Scripture in the very first chapter. Interestingly, there are almost identical statements in the London Baptist Confession of 1689 and the Philadelphia Baptist Confession of 1746.

So these statements are by no means simply confined to Anglicans or Presbyterians or Congregationalists, but all those in the mainstream of Reformed tradition would have affirmed the sufficiency of Scripture as it is outlined in the Westminster Confession. Here's what that confession says:

> The whole counsel of God concerning all things necessary for His own glory, man's salvation, faith and life, is either expressly set down in Scripture, or by good and necessary consequence may be deduced from Scripture: unto which nothing at any time is to be added, whether by new revelations of the Spirit, or traditions of men. (WCF 1:6)

Now, the issue of the sufficiency of Scripture was a major point of debate and disagreement in the Protestant Reformation. The Roman Catholic Church asserted that the Scriptures were not sufficient and authoritative in two particular ways.

First, the Roman Catholic Church argued that the Bible alone was insufficient to determine the canon, or the actual content, of the Scriptures. Roman Catholics believe that though the Bible may have been materially sufficient, it was not formally sufficient. This terminology may be unfamiliar; it has to do with a distinction that was common in those times that need not detain us here. Put simply, Rome argued that the church itself was necessary to determine the canon, or content, of Scripture.

Second, Rome believed that the Bible was not sufficient in itself to supply an adequate and infallible interpretation. Therefore, Catholics reasoned, the church was necessary in order to provide an inspired, inerrant, and infallible exposition of the Scriptures.

So Rome found the Bible to be insufficient in those ways. Over against that, the Protestant Reformers asserted that the Bible was sufficient for faith and life. They argued that the Bible was sufficient for the saints to know the way of salvation and the way of living with, for, and to God. They said the Bible provided everything Christians needed to know for salvation and sanctification, in other words.

This debate about the sufficiency of Scripture was exactly the topic that the apostle Paul addressed in 2 Timothy 3. So it's not surprising that when this debate raged in the church, this was one of the passages that the Protestant Reformers used to explain what they were asserting about the sufficiency of Scripture. In 2 Timothy 3:14–17, we read,

> But as for you, continue in what you have learned and have firmly believed, knowing from whom you learned it and how from childhood you have been acquainted with the sacred writings, which are able to make you wise for salvation through faith in Christ Jesus. All Scripture is breathed out by God and profitable for teaching, for reproof, for correction, and for training in righteousness, that the man of God may be competent, equipped for every good work.

Before we continue, it is necessary to set the context of this letter. It is the second of what are commonly called the Pastoral Epistles, which include 1 Timothy, 2 Timothy, and Titus. They are Paul's letters to pastors and church planters on themes pertaining to the responsibilities of pastoring and shepherding the church. They are major resources for the church from which to learn how to live and minister as believers today in our local congregations.

In these letters, then, Paul sets the priorities for healthy local bodies of Christians. And in 2 Timothy 3:14–17, Paul offers both an exhortation and an assertion regarding the proper foundation for Christian life, preaching, and ministry. And he offers this exhortation and this assertion to Timothy, a minister of the gospel and his son in Christ. Yet he offers this exhortation not only to Timothy, but to all ministers who serve in the name of Christ. Indeed, this exhortation is for all Christians.

The Exhortation: Live by the Book

The first exhortation Paul gives Timothy is this: Live by the Book. He says this in verses 14–15. Having just said in verse 12 that "all who desire to live a godly life in Christ Jesus will be persecuted," he goes on to say in verses 14 and 15, "continue in what you have learned and have firmly believed, knowing from whom you learned it and how from childhood you have been acquainted with the sacred writings, which are able to make you wise for salvation through faith in Christ Jesus."

The apostle Paul is here exhorting Timothy and the Ephesian Christians (and us) to continue, to persist, and to abide in the Scriptures because those Scriptures show us how to live the Christian life. Specifically, he is saying that those Scriptures

23

give us the wisdom that leads to salvation through faith that is in Jesus Christ. So he is asserting precisely the first part of what the Westminster Confession said regarding the sufficiency of Scripture—namely, that the Bible is sufficient to lead us into the wisdom and the knowledge that gives salvation, which is through faith in Jesus Christ. He is calling on Timothy to live and minister by the Book.

This is quite an extraordinary thing, because the apostle Paul was, after all, an apostle. He himself was a conduit of revelation. When he preached to the Thessalonians, he complimented them on the fact that they received his words not just as the words of men, but as the very words of God (see 1 Thess. 2:13). The Lord Jesus Christ had appointed him to serve as his own emissary, his own ambassador, having vested Paul with his own authority. The apostle Paul was able to do miracles. He was able to speak the very revelatory words of God. He was a vehicle of divine revelation. That's how much divine authority Paul's words carried.

It is therefore absolutely striking to see Paul here exhorting Timothy to live by the Book. Paul himself was an instrument of revelation, but he's pointing Timothy to the Book, to the Scriptures. Paul himself would write most of the New Testament, but he's pointing Timothy to the Book that already exists. In this instance, he is referring to the Hebrew Scriptures. Of course, ultimately what the apostle Paul says is applicable to the total canon of Scripture, both Old and New Testaments.

So he is pointing Timothy to the Book as the foundation of life. He is telling his young charge to continue, persist, and abide in the Scriptures. And isn't it striking that Paul here, speaking in the first instance about the Old Testament, can say to Timothy that the Hebrew Scriptures were sufficient? He is telling Timothy that the canon he had at the time was sufficient to give him the wisdom that leads to salvation, which is through faith in Jesus Christ. Amazingly, Paul is talking about the Old Testament.

Every once in a while, a Christian will ask a question such as this: "Were people saved in the Old Testament in the way we are saved today?" In other words, were people in the Old Testament saved by grace alone through faith alone in Christ alone? That question would never have occurred to the apostle Paul. When the apostle Paul wanted to prove the doctrine of salvation by grace alone through faith alone in Christ alone, where did he go? The Old Testament. In Romans, Paul goes right to the life of Abraham to prove justification by grace through faith (Rom. 4:1–3). And his point there is: "Friends, I'm not making this up. This is not some new teaching that I am bringing upon the church here. This is part of Scripture."

So the apostle Paul might have phrased the question this way: "Are we *still* saved by grace alone through faith alone in the promised Messiah alone, as they were in the Old Testament?" But he would never have asked the question whether the Old Testament saints were saved in the same way as we are today. This is because he drew his theology of grace from the Old Testament.

And he's telling Timothy the same thing. He is telling Timothy that the Bible he has—the Hebrew Scriptures—is able to give him the wisdom that leads to salvation through faith in Jesus Christ. So live and minister according to that Word, Timothy. Live by the Book.

An Assertion: The Bible Comes from God

But then, having given that exhortation, Paul does a second thing. He gives an assertion. Really, it's a triple assertion. It's an assertion about the Book that he's just asked Timothy to live by.

25

Since he calls Timothy to live by the Book, he tells him why he should live by the Book.

This is the second thing that Paul tells Timothy. He wants Timothy to live by the Book because its words come right from the mouth of God. Therefore, it is the most practical book in the world. It tells us how to live with God. Timothy was to continue and persist in the truth that he learned from the Scriptures because those Scriptures are three things—inspired, profitable, and the sufficient foundation for Christian living.

The Bible Is Inspired by God

We need to pay careful attention to what the apostle is saying here to Timothy. When the apostle Paul explains that the Scriptures are God-breathed, he is giving us the most important argument for the sufficiency of Scripture that we find in the Scriptures themselves. Very often, Roman Catholics will ask what verse in Scripture actually proves the sufficiency of Scripture. They will want a passage that makes it explicit that the Bible is sufficient for faith and life. There are, in fact, many places in Scripture that teach this doctrine; Paul is giving us one such place here.

But we must understand that, even apart from those passages, the most important point that proves the sufficiency of Scripture is understanding what Scripture, in fact, *is*. If the Bible is God's special revelation written, if it is the very Word of God to us, to call into question its sufficiency is to call into question the sufficiency of the very Word of God! What person in his right mind would want to call this into question? Who wants to stand up to God and say, "Your Word is not sufficient"? So if you understand what God's Word is in the first place, then you understand the most important point there is to understand about the sufficiency of Scripture. God's Word is adequate to do what he intends it to do.

Isaiah spoke of this sufficiency when he prophesied, "So shall my word be that goes out from my mouth; it shall not return to me empty, but it shall accomplish that which I purpose, and shall succeed in the thing for which I sent it" (Isa. 55:11). It never returns without doing what? Accomplishing what God set it out to accomplish. So the effectual power of God's Word is inherent in the Bible because it is God's Word. If you understand that God's Word is mighty, you understand the most important thing about the sufficiency of Scripture.

Moreover, the apostle Paul says that the Bible is inspired. It is the very Word of God. It is "breathed out by God"; that's the force of the Greek word that Paul uses here. You can feel the breath of God on your ear and in your heart as that Word is read in your hearing. It is an exceedingly precious thing. And that is why the people of God through the ages have valued the Word of God—it is God himself speaking to his people.

A number of years ago, my friend Mark Dever was lecturing in England at a conference on Puritan studies, and they were looking at the topic of the worship of God. He was trying to illustrate to his audience something of the value of the Word read and preached in the English language, book by book and verse by verse, to the first generation of English Christians under Protestant teaching. The people of God in those days had not had access to the Word of God in their own language in worship before the Reformation.

So Dr. Dever asked the participants whether they had ever been in a church building there in England where they saw a wrought-iron hook extending out from the pulpit. And a few of them had seen these. So he said, "Well, you can tell that that is from the early period of the Reformation in England." He then asked, "Does anybody here know what that hook was for?" And nobody raised a hand. He said, "Well, that was a holder for an hourglass. The hourglass was a gift from the congregation to their pastor. And if the congregation loved their pastor well, they would give him one or two turns of that hourglass."

Now, there was an audible gasp from a woman in the audience when she heard this. During the question-and-answer time, she asked Mark how, if the pastor preached for two or three hours, there was any time left for worship. This was not the question to ask Mark Dever, you understand! Also, as a historical aside, most Puritans didn't preach for two or three hours. Half an hour was a typical time for preaching, but in this case there were some congregations where pastors preached longer.

Dr. Dever first reminded the questioner and his audience that Puritans said that the hearing of the Word of God preached was the very apex of the service of worship. That is, it was an act of the highest worship to hear the Word of God. But then he pointed out what a privilege it was for the people of God to hear that Word read and proclaimed in their own language. And he answered the woman who had asked the question, "Ma'am, do you understand that those people who gave those hourglasses as gifts to their pastors would have remembered the smell of burning flesh in their nostrils from people who had been burned alive so that the Word of God could be read and explained to them in their own language? Therefore, they really didn't care much if the pastor took two or three hours to explain the Word of God." If we value the Word of God and realize what it is—the inspired word of the living God—we will have the same high estimation of it that the saints of which Dr. Dever spoke enjoyed.

So the apostle Paul here says to Timothy, "Live by the Book because it comes right out of God's mouth." What an enormous privilege to have the living Word of God in our own language! It reminds me of the story that J. I. Packer used to tell about the street evangelist who would put his hat down on the ground and dance around it to draw a crowd, saying, "It's alive! It's alive! It's alive!" He would then pick up his hat and there would be a Bible under it. Indeed, the Bible is the living Word of God. It is the very Word of God. It is not a dead letter; it is a living Word. It is from God's own mouth, and therefore it is sufficient.

The Bible Is Profitable

Second, the apostle Paul says that the Bible is profitable. It's the most practical book in the world. Sometimes Christians say things like, "All my pastor does is preach through Bible books; I wish he would teach something practical." Paul tells Timothy that the Bible tells us everything we need to know about salvation and sanctification, evangelism and edification, faith and life. How practical is that? Notice how Paul puts it: "All Scripture is breathed out by God and profitable for teaching, for reproof, for correction, and for training in righteousness" (2 Tim. 3:16).

It's profitable for teaching, for instruction, for imparting the truth of God's Word. It's profitable for grounding the people of God in the knowledge of the truth. It's profitable for reproof or admonition. It's profitable for warning the people of God. The Word of God, speaking against errors in both belief and behavior, is profitable for correction and for redirecting. This is the positive side of the warning.

It is also profitable for training in righteousness. The Scriptures are profitable for four things, then: teaching, reproof, correction, and training in righteousness. We could put it this way: The Scriptures are profitable for discipline, discipling, and preparing believers to live in godliness.

Put in popular terms, the apostle Paul is saying that the Bible is inherently practical. It is not your pastor's job to make it practical. It already is. It's the most practical book in the world. And the only reason we think it's impractical to hear the Word of God expounded is that we're interested in other questions and other things. It is the questions addressed and the things spoken of in the Word of God that are truly practical. And if we are interested in other questions and other things, we're interested in the wrong things, because there is nothing impractical in the Bible from Genesis to Revelation. As Jesus said, quoting Deuteronomy 8:3, "Man shall not live by bread alone, but by every word that comes from the mouth of God" (Matt. 4:4).

So the apostle Paul is saying, "Timothy, this book is practical. It shows you how to live the Christian life. It shows you the way of salvation." Now, in verse 16, Paul says that it shows us the way to live the Christian life. It's practical and profitable for living the Christian life.

Let me again summarize the position of the historic Reformed confessions: the Bible contains the whole counsel of God concerning all things necessary for his own glory and for man's salvation, faith, and life. The framers of these confessions, whose language was nearly identical on this matter, are simply summarizing what the apostle Paul has just said in 2 Timothy 3:14–16. The Bible is sufficient, practical, and profitable for salvation and life. It shows us the way to live as Christians.

Paul's teachings to Timothy here are not unusual. He frequently says such things. Two examples must suffice.

First, look at Romans 15:4. Here, at the end of that glorious book of Romans in what is considered the "practical" or ethical section of this book, Paul says, "For whatever was written in former days was written for our instruction, that through endurance and through the encouragement of the Scriptures we might have hope." Notice, then, what Paul is saying to the church at Rome. He is telling them that the Scriptures were given for our encouragement and for our hope. They are there for the living of the Christian life, for encouraging us to love and good deeds, for giving us hope for living our lives.

Second, let us look at 1 Corinthians 10:1–12. Twice in this passage Paul delivers thunderous words of truth about the Old Testament:

> For I want you to know, brothers, that our fathers were all under the cloud, and all passed through the sea, and all were baptized into Moses in the cloud and in the sea, and all ate the same spiritual food, and all drank the same spiritual drink. For they drank from the spiritual Rock that followed them, and the Rock was Christ. Nevertheless, with most of them God was not pleased, for they were overthrown in the wilderness.
>
> Now these things took place as examples for us, that we might not desire evil as they did. Do not be idolaters as some of them were; as it is written [in Exodus 32:6], "The people sat down to eat and drink and rose up to play." We must not indulge in sexual immorality as some of them did, and twenty-three thousand fell in a single day. We must not put Christ to the test, as some of them did and were destroyed by serpents, nor grumble, as some of them did and were destroyed by the Destroyer. Now these things happened to them as an example, but they were written down for our instruction, on whom the end of the ages has come. Therefore let anyone who thinks that he stands take heed lest he fall.

Paul's words are absolutely staggering. He is saying that the events of the wilderness in the life of the people of the nation of Israel occurred by God's appointment for our instruction.

Twenty-three thousand people died in one day so that you and I would learn not to grumble, or complain, or follow after false gods! Paul says that these things happened so that you and I would learn to respond in faith to the Word and promises of God.

This was an exceedingly costly lesson of instruction. Not only did these things happen, but they were written down for our instruction. The apostle Paul is constantly pointing to the practicality of Scripture. It is for the purpose of teaching us, reproving us, correcting us, rebuking us, admonishing us, and discipling us. It's a practical, profitable book that is authoritative and fully adequate to equip us to live the Christian life.

The idea is that the Bible is inherently practical and profitable. It is designed for our profit, our good, our use, and our benefit. The Bible is inspired. It's from the mouth of God, and it's the most practical book in the world.

The Sufficient Foundation for Christian Living

This brings us to our third point. We see it there in 2 Timothy 3:16–17:

> All Scripture is breathed out by God and profitable for teaching, for reproof, for correction, and for training in righteousness, that the man of God may be competent, equipped for every good work.

The Bible is profitable to produce a fully equipped, godly Christian man or woman, who is ready to live with God, for God, and to God, to do every good work in accordance with God's Word. The Bible is sufficient for salvation and for sanctification. So our third point is that the Bible is the sufficient foundation for Christian living.

It's precisely at this point, of course, that the Roman Catholic Church attacked the Protestant Reformers. And it's precisely this point that was asserted by the Protestant Reformers over against the Roman Catholic Church. The Reformers argued that the Bible itself brought the people of God into being. The Roman Catholics said just the opposite: the church determines the content of the Bible. Therefore, in that sense, the church created the Bible. The Reformers replied, in effect, "Nonsense. The people of God never create the Word of God; the Word of God always creates the people of God. It's always been that way."

A brief survey of Scripture bears out the Reformers' convictions. For instance, Abraham did not create the people of God in Genesis 12:1–3, when he was called to be the father of the faithful. Rather, God's Word came to Abraham and called him out of darkness into great light and made him to be a people.

Or think about the people of Israel after the exodus. God's people at Sinai did not create themselves. God's Word created the people of God at Sinai as the ten words were announced and God's grace was set forth for them. God's Word created a people out of what had not been a people.

Of course, we could cite many more instances, but the two above are paradigmatic and therefore programmatic. That is just to say that God's Word always creates his people—this is the biblical pattern. Just as God's Word called the world into being, so God's Word calls the church into being. The church is never before the Word; the church is created *by* the Word.

The Word Recognized by the Church

To be sure, the Protestant Reformers acknowledged the fact that the church had the responsibility (especially given the fact that

false writings were being attributed to the apostles) to acknowledge which books it received as the inspired Word of God. And
it looked for two qualifications in all those books that would be
ultimately recognized as the New Testament canon: the mark of
inspiration and the mark of apostolicity. This simply means that
the doctrine of the book in question had to be in accord with
the doctrine of the accepted canon of Scripture, the rule of faith.

In addition to this, the book in question had to have come
from the authentic apostolic circle. This does not mean that it
had to be written directly by an apostle. It did mean that it was
written under the influence of an apostle in the apostolic circle.
For example, Luke himself was not an apostle, but he was an
affiliate and friend of the apostle Paul. Similarly, Mark may not
have been an apostle, but it was often assumed that Peter was
behind the Gospel of Mark. And so the early church looked
for these marks of inspiration and apostolicity. By so doing, the
church simply recognized but did not create the canon.

So the church was not necessary to bring the Word of God
into being. The Word of God brought the church into being. The
church recognized and acknowledged what was the true Word
of God, the canon. This is what the Reformers urged against
the Church of Rome's denial of the sufficiency of Scripture in
terms of the canon.

Rome replied, however, that if you commit to an inspired
Bible that does not have an authoritative, infallible interpretation from the church, then the church will end up with all
sorts of crazy opinions. It will have hundreds of different views.
The Reformers acknowledged that very real problem, but they
responded by saying this: Scripture is clear. It is so clear about
what it teaches about salvation and the way of the Christian life
that we dare not attempt to add to it some supposedly inspired
interpretation of the church that usurps its unique authority to

speak into the lives of God's people. In essence, they said that Rome was calling into question the sufficiency of God's Word to accomplish what Paul said it would in all the people of God here in 2 Timothy 3:14–17.

This is why, by the way, during the high Middle Ages, the Roman Catholic Church did not allow the average person in the pew to read the Bible. Incredibly, during the Inquisition, the Bible was put on the list of indexed books. The index was not a very fancy Library of Congress card-catalogue classification system. The list of indexed books was the list of books that Catholics were forbidden to read. Why? Because, as a good Catholic, one needed to listen to the interpretation of the church. The average person didn't need to read the Bible for himself, Rome argued.

Over against all this kind of reasoning, the Reformers affirmed that the Bible was perspicuous. It has the quality of clarity; it is so clear in what it says about salvation and life that that Word must be brought to bear directly on the souls of believers, because it is that Word that engenders life and godliness. Therefore, the average person in the pew can read and understand the clear Word of God without the additional aid of the supposedly infallible teaching office of the Roman Catholic Church.

The Lord Jesus Christ on the Sufficiency of the Word

We've been studying what Paul has to say about this issue. But, of course, it's not just Paul. Jesus makes the same point. In Luke 16:17, Jesus says: "But it is easier for heaven and earth to pass away than for one dot of the Law to become void." In the context of Luke 16, Jesus has introduced a statement that affirms the eternally abiding validity of the Word of God. Immediately upon the heels of that assertion comes the interesting story of the rich man and Lazarus.

A poor man named Lazarus, who endured the slings and arrows of outrageous fortune, dies and goes to Abraham's bosom. The rich man, however, dies and enters into the torment of Hades. A conversation ensues. We read in verse 24, beginning with the rich man:

> And he called out, "Father Abraham, have mercy on me, and send Lazarus to dip the end of his finger in water and cool my tongue, for I am in anguish in this flame." But Abraham said, "Child, remember that you in your lifetime received your good things, and Lazarus in like manner bad things; but now he is comforted here, and you are in anguish. And besides all this, between us and you a great chasm has been fixed, in order that those who would pass from here to you may not be able, and none may cross from there to us." And he said, "Then I beg you, father, to send him to my father's house—for I have five brothers—so that he may warn them, lest they also come into this place of torment." But Abraham said, "They have Moses and the Prophets; let them hear them." (Luke 16:24–29)

The rich man says, in effect, "Look, send someone back from the dead to tell my brothers so that they'll turn and repent of their sins." And Jesus' response, put into the mouth of father Abraham, is: "They have Moses and the Prophets; let them hear them."

What is Jesus saying? He is basically telling the rich man (and all of us) that the Scriptures are sufficient to show the way of salvation. No miracle is needed, such as Lazarus coming back from the dead to tell people about the afterlife. What we need to do is to go to the Bible, because the Bible is sufficient. That's Jesus' message.

What does the rich man reply to all of this? Look at verses 30–31: "And he said, 'No, father Abraham, but if someone goes to them from the dead, they will repent.' He said to him, 'If they do not hear Moses and the Prophets, neither will they be convinced if someone should rise from the dead.'" Isn't it interesting that Jesus has the man in hell saying that the Bible is not enough, that Scripture is not sufficient to show the way of salvation?

The conclusion is this: live by the Book, because the Bible is from the mouth of God. It's the most practical book in the world. It is profitable for living the Christian life. It is fully adequate and authoritative for the purpose God gave it. It needs nothing added to it to equip you for every good work, for the living of the Christian life.

This is the charter of Christian freedom. No man can say to you:

- the Bible plus whatever secret I have discovered;
- the Bible plus whatever command I have added;
- the Bible plus whatever new revelation I have had;
- the Bible plus the new program that I have.

It's the Bible *alone*. We live by God's Word, by Jesus' Word. It sets us free from all the doctrines and commandments of men. True freedom is to hear the Word of our Maker, Defender, Redeemer, and Friend, and to live in the freedom of that Word that is for his glory and our good.

3

The Truth of God

R. C. SPROUL

*For this purpose I was born and for this purpose I
have come into the world—to bear witness to the
truth. Everyone who is of the truth listens to my
voice. (John 18:37)*

I RECALL A TIME that I was cornered by a man who
had an interesting career in the academic world (he had been
a professor at MIT), as well as the scientific community. He
began to ask me questions related to apologetics and the truth
claims of Christianity. And at one point in this discussion he
said, "You guys"—meaning the clergy—"are always preaching in
church on Sunday and telling people to make decisions and to
give their hearts to Jesus, yet you won't defend the truth claims
toward which you are calling people to commit their very lives."

The man expressed a valid frustration, I think. In the church, of all places, there seems to be a facility for ignoring the foundation of truth as it relates to the Christian faith. I hear people say, "I am not a Christian because I don't feel the need for Christianity," as if all we are involved with is some kind of popular psychology. We are not here as Christians to proclaim that which will make people feel good. We are here to proclaim and to declare reality. We are here to proclaim the truth.

The notion that we should believe something not because it's true but because of how we feel about it was brought home vividly to me a number of years ago. I remember being at a conference for clergy where someone was presenting a report on the demographics of the American society, compiled by some agency. This report detailed the shift that is apparent and measurable in our nation regarding how we arrive at what we believe is true. Fascinatingly, it argued that we as a nation have been conditioned, almost like Pavlov's dogs, to respond not to argumentation or to evidence, but rather to impressions, usually couched in some form of entertainment.

Pilate's Question: The Crisis of Our Time

But Jesus did not think about truth the way we as a nation seem to. The Lord Jesus Christ was on trial for his life in front of the politically enterprising Pontius Pilate, who asked him, "What is truth?" (John 18:38). The question was basically this: "Jesus, what is this all about? Who are you? Your people have delivered you into my hands, with a claim of sedition, saying that you are trying to establish some kind of kingdom. Are your motives and your plans strictly political? Are you the king of the Jews?" In effect, Jesus answered, "That's what you say. The kingdom that I'm talking about, Pilate, is not of this world. It is for this reason that I have come into the world, to bear witness to the truth. That's why I'm here" (see 18:36). And then Jesus makes an astonishing statement: "Everyone who is of the truth listens to my voice" (18:37).

How often do we think about the fact that Jesus' purpose in coming into the world was to bear witness to the truth? Our Lord himself had a passion for the truth. He was prepared to die for the truth. He saw his mission in the incarnation to bear witness to the truth. How is it possible that in any Christian community we could ever take a cavalier attitude toward truth, when bearing witness to the truth was at the very heart of our Savior's mission? We cannot afford to take the truth lightly.

Why do Christians argue over minor points of theology? The good news is that we argue about seemingly small things because we understand that truth is important. Truth is something that flows out of the very character of God. To put it bluntly: every time we distort the truth, we distort our understanding of who God is. Jesus never distorted the truth; he came to bear witness to it.

What was Pilate's response to Jesus? It was a question. He simply asked, "What is truth?" Sometimes it distresses me that the Bible records conversations such as these with such an economy of language. I would have loved to see how Pilate actually asked that question. What was his attitude? What was the inflection of his voice when he stood before Jesus and asked, "What is truth?" Was Pilate being cynical? Did he sound like a skeptic who, when Jesus said, "I came to bear witness to the truth," laughed and said, "Ha, ha, ha, what's truth?" Or perhaps for one moment in his political life, did he become pensive? Did he put away the public-opinion polls and say to Jesus with all earnestness, "What is the truth? Really, what *is* truth?"

Now, if Pilate had followed through with the latter scenario, the trial would have turned out differently. The irony of this situation is that when Pontius Pilate asked his question concerning truth, the very incarnation of truth was standing there in front of him. Jesus could have said, "Remember what I said just the other night. I am truth. You want to know what the truth is? Follow me. Continue in my Word, and then, Pilate, you will know the truth. And the truth will set you free" (cf. John 14:6; 8:32).

Apparently, however, Jesus did not engage in a moment of pedagogy in response to Pilate's question. Immediately after asking this question, Pilate went out and spoke the truest statement he had ever uttered when he said, "I find no fault in this man" (John 18:38 KJV). That was the unvarnished truth. But having said it, he couldn't live with it, and he caved in to the spirit of pragmatism that finds truth not in objective reality, but in what is personally and politically expedient. I don't think there's a greater crisis in our age than the crisis that surrounds Pilate's question "What is truth?"

A Correspondence Theory of Truth?

Dr. Francis Schaeffer was fond of speaking of what he called "true truth." I remember that it used to provoke some laughter and amusement that somebody would walk around in knickers talking about "true truth." Well, Francis Schaeffer didn't stutter. When Francis Schaeffer spoke about "true truth," he was not surrendering to redundancy. Dr. Schaeffer understood that there is a battle going on about the very nature of truth. What Schaeffer was saying is that there is a truth that is real and not reduced to my own subjective preferences. Schaeffer was speaking to a generation that had bought in to a relativistic view of truth, which declares that something is true for you if it works for you, if it means something to you. If the same "truth" doesn't do the same for me, that's okay. In other words, it's all relative.

My favorite illustration of this phenomenon is of a college student that I spoke with some years ago. She said to me, "R. C., if you believe in God, and your faith in God means something to you, then for you, God is true. But I don't feel the need to believe in God; I don't feel the need for religion. I'm perfectly happy and content with my life the way it is. So for me there is no God. We can certainly get along as friends and agree to disagree. For you there is a God; for me there is no God. So we can have peace."

When this happens, a corpse named *truth* lies in the streets. So I said, "I don't think you understand what I'm saying. I'm talking to you about a God who is objectively true. If this God that I am talking about does not exist, all my praying, all my worship, all my ministry, all my devotion cannot possibly conjure him up. God may have the ability to create me, but I don't have the ability to create God out of nothing. Conversely, if you don't believe in God, and you don't find worship or prayer or any of those things meaningful, the God I'm talking about is the kind of God that all your unbelief cannot destroy. We're talking about truth, not about personal preferences or what turns you or me on."

In that discussion, I took a view of truth that is in danger not only of being obscured, but of being totally eclipsed. It's a view of truth that has historically been called a correspondence view of truth. This simply means that truth is that which corresponds to reality. The correspondence theory of truth is a statement of objective truth. What is real is true. Truth is that which corresponds to reality.

43

Then the next generation came along, saying to John Locke (one of the philosophers who defended this view in the seventeenth century), "But wait a minute. We have to ask the next question. Truth is that which corresponds to reality, as perceived by whom?" And I'll date myself with this illustration, but some readers will recall the famous slogan of the sportscaster Howard Cosell. He used to say, "Tell it like it is." You didn't know that Howard Cosell was a prophet, did you?

In all seriousness, if we leave our definition of truth as that which corresponds to reality, without qualifying this statement, we may still find ourselves in a sea of subjectivism, with rivaling Cosells arguing about how it really is.

The Truth about Truth

At the heart of Christianity is the proper view of the correspondence of truth, namely, that truth is that which corresponds to reality *as it is perceived by God.* The reason we add that qualifier is that we understand that God and God alone has an absolutely comprehensive, infallible view of reality. Only God has the ability to speak from what the philosophers call "the viewpoint or the vantage point of eternity." He alone sees the end from the beginning. Only God perceives all the mitigating circumstances and sees the whole picture. No matter how brilliant we are, no matter how knowledgeable we are, there are severe limits to our scope of understanding.

I saw this many years ago in a mainline denomination's report on human sexuality. This denomination had the audacity to declare that, in its opinion, premarital sexual activity was healthy and acceptable. It even went so far as to argue that, under certain circumstances, extramarital activity could be helpful to the establishment of a sound marriage. The report contained a host of citations from authorities to support this view, from this psychiatrist and that psychologist.

Do you see what happened there? Humans studied the matter, and since they knew so much about what is good for humanity, they concluded that something that the Bible specifically condemns as wrong was, in fact, good for us. When the church trades in its infallible source of truth, the Scriptures, for the source of human opinion, we no longer understand truth; we are back again in the shadows of mere human opinion.

Some years ago, we put on a conference in western Pennsylvania on the inerrancy of Scripture. On this occasion, I prepared an essay on the biblical concept of truth. To do it scientifically, I went to the scholarly sources and studied lexicography and word usage and things of that nature. I looked up a technical scholarly essay on the ancient meaning of the Greek word *aletheia*, which is the New Testament word for *truth*. I looked at a study of how the term *truth* functioned in New Testament documents, as well as first-century Greek documents, earlier Greek statements of Plato, Socrates, Euripides, and so on. I studied how the word was used in the Septuagint and even in the later church fathers. They gave a crystallized definition of the meaning of the term *aletheia*. The first thing that was said about it was that, biblically at least, the term refers to "real states of affairs." Thus, the Bible is committed to an objective view of truth.

Now, the irony of this particular study was the identity of the author, whose name appeared at the end of the article. It was none other than Rudolf Bultmann, who was one of the towering figures of New Testament scholarship in the twentieth century. He didn't believe in a view of objective truth at all, but at least he recognized that the truth he opposed was indeed the biblical concept of truth: real states of affairs.

The Implications of the Truth of God's Word

When we talk about a correspondence view of truth whereby we define truth as that which corresponds to reality as given to us by God, we're not participating in simply an abstract investigation of philosophical matters. This view has massive ramifications and consequences for us as people in our daily lives. Here are some of the implications, as I see them.

First, let's start with the good news. The good news is that on the day of judgment, God will judge the entire world—every event, every incident, every national crisis, and every personal crisis—according to the truth. He won't have to deliberate and give his opinions over to a jury, to have them debate on what the truth is. Nobody will be voting on what the truth is, for God will give a perfect verdict of truth.

Have you ever wondered why the Bible uses the imagery of silence and closed mouths (cf. Hab. 2:20; Rom. 3:19; Rev. 8:1) when it speaks of the judgment day? I'm convinced that it's because the truth of God's judgment will be so utterly manifest that even the most obstreperous human being will recognize the utter futility of further debate. When God exercises and utters his judgment, the debate is over. Why? Because the truth has been spoken by the One who knows the truth perfectly.

There are many times that we meet with people who know far more than we do about certain things. And many times, it feels as though we enter in where angels fear to tread when we argue with them. Such was the case with me when I used to do that with my mentor, John Gerstner! But I will go on record by saying that even Gerstner can be wrong. I don't know where, but I have to affirm the possibility! So that at least excuses me in part from my willingness to argue with him. But who will contend with the Almighty? Who has been his guide or counselor? As I've heard Eric Alexander say, "Who is going to correct the viewpoint of God?"

There's another element of good news, and it has to do with the Bible. There are those who say that the Bible represents nothing more than the insights and the opinions of primitive, prescientific ancient Jews. To the degree that such views have any significance for us today, it is in a historical capacity, but that's all. No normative authority in the Bible can bind the conscience of a human being, because it is merely and completely the words of men. Now, beloved, if the Bible is simply the words of men, then it has no claim on your conscience. It cannot bind you to an ultimate obligation. I can understand that, if we grant the premise of that argument.

Here's what I can't understand: I can't understand people who tell me that the Bible is the Word of God and it can err, but the truth of God cannot err. In other words, in this view, the Bible is the Word of God, but it is not the truth of God. That is just nonsense. If this is God's Word, if God inspired this Word, it is unthinkable that the God who is the Truth could ever inspire falsehood and if it is the inspired Word of God, then we have the truth.

I remember taking a course in seminary on Christian education. The professor gave us an assignment to make up a creative Sunday school lesson for children. I didn't know what else to do, so I designed a very simple crossword puzzle. The purpose of this was to make the learning of these principles something of a game—to make learning entertaining. Oh, did that professor come down on my head! He said, "Don't you realize what you just communicated to these children?" And I said, "No, sir. What's that?" He replied, "By using this crossword puzzle, you are suggesting that life is a puzzle and the church has all the answers."

This reminded me of Paul's words to Timothy. Men like this professor were "always learning and never able to arrive at a knowledge of the truth" (2 Tim. 3:7). This same professor then went on to give us a lecture about how truth is a pursuit. For this man, that's what real scholarship was: simply pursuing the truth. But we never reach conclusions. So I asked him, "Well, then, what am I doing here, in seminary?" He didn't really have an answer for that.

In all of this, I didn't mean to suggest to the children that the church has all the answers, because we confess that the church doesn't have all the answers. We know that our knowledge of God is not comprehensive or exhaustive. There is still an element of truth that we do not apprehend, for we see in the mirror darkly (see 1 Cor. 13:12). That is the profession of Christianity. But what God has revealed to us, as Martin Luther once said somewhere, "is more certain than life itself." Or, as Luther said elsewhere, *Spiritus sanctus non est scepticus*: "The Holy Spirit is not a skeptic." As Christians, then, we believe that the fountainhead of all truth has been given to us in God's Word, the Bible, of which Jesus said, "Thy word is truth" (John 17:17 KJV).

God's Truth: Propositional *and* Personal

In closing, I want to add this caveat: the biblical concept of truth means much more than simple propositions. It does not mean less, to be sure, but it certainly means more. Again, I don't ever want to negotiate propositional truth or objective truth, but we have to understand that in addition to the fact that the biblical concept of truth refers to real states of affairs, the Bible also declares that truth is *personal*. Truth, according to God's Word, is very much involved with personal relationships.

Today in the church, we have people who teach what is called *relational theology*, which is willing to trade in objective truth and propositional truth. They teach that the only thing that matters is personal relationships. The questions they want to ask are: "Are we treating each other properly? Are we being loving? Are we being nice? Are we being kind to one another?" This is the kind of attitude that says, "Don't talk to me about doctrine; talk to me about people."

That's a false dichotomy. In the biblical view of truth, God speaks to us in propositions that are true, and that same God commands us to exercise truth in our personal relationships. In fact, the history of our relationship to God as redeemed sinners is based on God's concept of "doing the truth," as well as speaking the truth.

Think for a minute of your own life, and think of how many times your life has been violated or wounded because somebody you trusted was unfaithful. A man once said to me in private, "My hope for my life is that when I die there will be five people who will come to my funeral and will be able to sit there without looking at their watches." That may sound grim. But all of this stems from the fact that we're frightened to let anybody know us to such a degree that we have to put our trust in that person, because we are still ashamed to be known. In fact, there's only one person who knows me perfectly with whom I'm still able to enjoy a comfortable relationship even though he does know me perfectly. That person is my Savior, Jesus Christ.

You see, the whole basis for our relationship to God is trust. We're justified by faith, and faith is an active form of doing the truth. It is an active form of trusting someone to keep his word. Jesus says he must go to the cross and his disciples say to him, "You can't do that. We'll go get our swords. Don't go to Jerusalem. That's no way; we can't possibly be saved by a dead Messiah." Jesus said, "Trust me." He was and is trustworthy.

The Bible tells us that we're related to God by a covenant. At the heart of a covenant is a promise. I don't give a lot of attention to people who make promises to me who have no regard for truth, but because God is truth, his promises are absolutely trustworthy.

Thus, what is at stake in this entire battle for truth is nothing less than faith itself. It is not that faith is something that is divorced from truth. Rather, truth is the very foundation of faith. If truth is not the foundation, then we are left with credulity, with superstition. We are left with something like magic. Whatever else we have, if truth is not the foundation of our faith, we do not have Christianity. God doesn't say to us, "I'm utterly untrustworthy, but it's okay—I don't care about the truth anyway. Truth is whatever you want it to be. Believe therefore in me." No, no, no! He says, "I want you to believe on me because I am the truth."

And if he is not the truth, then he is not worthy of your faith. He's not worthy of your worship. The Bible takes a dim view of worshiping that which is false—see, for instance, Isaiah 44:9–19, where the prophet mocks the inability of false gods. So why, my beloved, are we afraid of truth? If Christianity is based on truth, and if truth is of the nature and character of God, and Christ is the very incarnation of the truth, what truth can possibly harm us? Everyone who is of the truth hears the voice of God. Whose voice do you hear?

4

Scripture Alone

JAMES M. BOICE

*[Know] this first of all, that scoffers will come in
the last days with scoffing, following their own
sinful desires. They will say, "Where is the promise
of his coming? For ever since the fathers fell asleep,
all things are continuing as they were from the
beginning of creation." (2 Peter 3:3–4)*

I HAD THE PRIVILEGE of chairing the International
Council on Biblical Inerrancy (ICBI), and often I receive questions from people in churches regarding this work. Perhaps the
most frequent question is: "Does the church's doctrine of Scripture matter that much?" The argument goes like this: "God
is doing his work, and he's doing it in all kinds of churches.
Therefore, does it really matter whether we have that high view

of Scripture that the church has always had? Perhaps it's all right to have a quite lesser view now."

Well, one perfectly valid answer to these questions is this: the church's doctrine of Scripture mattered to the Reformers. Not only did they believe it as a matter of doctrine, they lived it as a matter of life. So much so was this the case that, for the sake of the Word of God, they were quite willing to suffer the loss of all things.

Martin Luther put it like this in the great hymn of the Reformation, which we sing many times: "Let goods and kindred go, this mortal life also; the body they may kill: God's truth abideth still; his kingdom is forever."[1] And on the basis of the conviction that the Bible is the Word of God and is therefore truthful and trustworthy (because God is truthful and trustworthy), they were willing even to lose their lives. If we contrast that high view of Scripture with the exceedingly low view of the church today, it is certainly worth asking if it might not be the case that the weakness of the church in our time comes from a lack of exactly the conviction that the Reformers had.

Calvin and Luther on Scripture

Now, I don't want to spend the following pages merely quoting the Reformers (though we would surely benefit if I did just that!), but let me cite just a few. Luther wrote in his great preface to the Old Testament:

I beg and faithfully warn every pious Christian not to stumble at the simplicity of the language and stories that will often meet him there. He should not doubt that, however simple

1. Martin Luther, "A Mighty Fortress Is Our God" (1529).

they may seem, these are the very words, works, judgments and deeds of the high majesty and wisdom of God.[2]

Again, in his famous "table talk," he said:

We must make a great difference between God's word and the word of man. A man's word is a little sound that flies into the air, and soon vanishes; but the word of God is greater than heaven and earth, yea, greater than death and hell, for it forms part of the power of God, and endures everlastingly.[3]

And then this quote from John Calvin in his commentary on 2 Timothy 3:16:

This is a principle which distinguishes our religion from all others, that we know that God hath spoken to us, and are fully convinced that the prophets did not speak of their own suggestion, but that being organs of the Holy Spirit, they only uttered what they had been commissioned from heaven to declare. Whoever then wishes to profit in the scriptures, let him, first of all, lay down this as a settled point, that the Law and the Prophets are not a doctrine delivered according to the will and pleasure of men, but dictated by the Holy Spirit.[4]

It is truly a wonderful theological exercise to spend some time reading through the Reformers to see what they said about the

2. Martin Luther, "Preface to the Old Testament," in *What Luther Says: An Anthology*, comp. Ewald M. Plass, vol. 1 (St. Louis: Concordia Publishing House, 1959), 71.

3. Martin Luther, Table Talk 44, in *A Compend of Luther's Theology*, ed. Hugh Thompson Kerr (Philadelphia: Westminster Press, 1943), 10.

4. John Calvin, *Commentary on II Timothy*, trans. William Pringle (Grand Rapids: Baker, 2003), 248–49.

Bible and then to contrast their sentiments with the kind of weak statements that we so often hear in our own time.

The point I want to make is that we need the conviction of the Reformers today. It is out of the belief and certainty that God has spoken in Scripture that the strength comes for a church to be truly effective in the world. It is our strength as Christians, too.

The Importance of a Place to Stand

I must admit to having been surprised at the number of places where one can actually teach a high view of Scripture and receive a good response. Some years ago now, when the work of the ICBI was just getting underway, I received an invitation from Princeton Theological Seminary to come and speak about inerrancy. It didn't come from the faculty; it came from a group of evangelical students that were at the seminary. And even though it had come from that source, I must confess that Princeton was the place that I was least eager to go and speak about inerrancy. I had gone there as a student myself. I knew the faculty; they knew me. I knew their convictions; they knew mine.

I could imagine a very embarrassing situation. I envisioned arriving there at the invitation of what I assumed to be five or six evangelicals and being confronted by them plus thirty of my former professors, all of whom had many learned degrees and who, after I gave my initial presentation, would begin to ask me questions about things I knew absolutely nothing about. Now, that is not easy under any circumstances! But certainly, in an academic setting like that, I imagined them saying to me, "Dr. Boice"—I was hoping they wouldn't call me "Jimmy"—"tell us what you think about so-and-so's article." They would then proceed to read something out of the latest journal, which, of course, I would not have read. And I did not know what to do about that fear. I thought the invitation deserved the honor of a response, but I did not want to go.

Then I remembered something that I had learned years ago when I first began to do question-and-answer sessions. I learned that it is always good to have someone else with you. If you know the answer to the question, you can answer it and everybody thinks you're brilliant. And if you don't know the answer, well, you defer to your friend and everyone thinks you're humble! So I thought to myself, "Who could really help me out in this situation?" Almost at once, I thought of Dr. John Gerstner. If anyone could handle himself in a debate, it was John Gerstner. So he graciously drove the whole way across the state to be there and, in fact, arrived at Princeton before I did. He was already engaged in debate when I got there, about an hour early.

Now, the format of this particular engagement was a sort of lunch meeting that the conservative group of students hosted. We met at 12 o'clock, we ate until about 12:30, and then we began to talk. We had forty-five minutes to speak, and then the last fifteen minutes were open for questions, and everybody would leave at 1:30. I divided my time with Dr. Gerstner. I presented maybe twenty minutes, and he did another twenty minutes. And then we opened it up for questions.

We had two great surprises. The first was that so many people had come. There were no hostile professors (I think such a meeting was thought to be very obviously beneath them). But about four hundred students came. Obviously, they were very concerned about the matter of the authority of the Scriptures. Now, by no means were they in our camp. They were on the other side. They were trying to argue, for the most part, that what you believe about the Bible really

55

doesn't matter; rather, what matters is your experience of Christ. This, of course, is not unimportant. But we will deal with it more fully below.

The second thing that surprised me was that these four hundred or so students stayed and asked questions. After an hour they were still there. After two hours they were still there. They were beginning to trickle away after three hours. And it wasn't until 4 o'clock in the afternoon that we were actually able to bring that session to a close.

The debate had been very rapid-fire, and Dr. Gerstner certainly did his part. And afterward I went away thinking to myself, "Well, at least we did our duty. I don't think we changed any minds, but they have at least been exposed to a conservative point of view." Two days later I got a letter from one of the students who had been there. He wrote a very interesting comment. Let me quote it at length:

> I have never held to the doctrine of inerrancy, and yet I found myself siding with the two of you as today's discussion proceeded. Isn't it true that behind most of the questions you received was a crypto-cultural Christianity? That is, there seemed to be a secret capitulation to the "try it, you'll like it" mentality of our civilization. That's how it seemed to me. Those questioners did not really seem to be engaged in a point-to-point argument over any substantial theological issue. Rather, most seemed to think that to preach the gospel in our day and age, one doesn't need a place to stand. All one has to do is stand in the pulpit and say, not, "Thus saith the Lord," but only "Try it, you'll like it." I'm surprised that I found myself saying you were right and all of us were wrong insofar as this very basic point is concerned: why we stand where we stand makes all the difference in the world.

Remember, this is coming from a person who started out opposed to inerrancy. But as he faced the issue of the authority of Scripture and examined it in the light of the experience of the church, he came to see that it makes all the difference in the world whether God has really spoken in this Bible and done so truthfully. Now, of course, that's what the Reformers discovered and believed. And it was certainly one of the fundamental strengths, if not *the* fundamental strength, of the Protestant Reformation.

The Problem of Tradition

Now I would like to think about the way in which the Reformers grappled with this problem in their time, particularly because we have some distortions regarding their view in current popular thinking. We often say (in the Protestant church, at least) that the Reformers believed in the Bible and the Roman church did not. Of course that is not true. The Reformers "rediscovered" the Bible, if I can put it like that. The Roman church, when it began to rediscover the Bible, partially through the teachings of the Reformers, discovered that it didn't like exactly what was there. So it made some adjustments in its theology in order to keep its traditions. But in the beginning, at least in theory, the Roman church, as well as the Protestant church, believed that the Bible was the Word of God and that God had spoken in it truthfully.

What the Reformers were doing in their formulation of the doctrine of Scripture was really fighting a battle on two fronts. On the one hand, they had the Roman church with its traditions. So they had to talk about the place of Scripture over against the corrupt traditions of men. On the other hand, particularly as the Reformation got underway, they were faced with the eccentricities of the enthusiasts or the pietists of the day. So they had to talk to these people about the Word of God and the Spirit and how the two of them operate together. And the answers they gave to both groups went together to make up their doctrine of Scripture.

Now, in terms of the tradition of the church, which they had inherited in part from the Roman church of the Middle Ages, the principle was this: In both the Roman church and the Protestant communions it was understood, and rightly so, that there are traditions in the church and that these are not necessarily bad. Some of them may be bad and some may be good; some may be utterly indifferent.

Thus, in the early days of the Reformation, the proper relationship between Scripture and tradition would be understood in this way: Scripture, being the Word of God, was the sole authority; and tradition, being that which man has produced, was something that was worth listening to and learning from. On this (correct) view, tradition was obviously subordinated to the Word of God, which alone is absolutely trustworthy.

What happened, of course, was that the Reformers began to discover Scripture. They began to read it. They began to find out what its teachings were, beginning with the great doctrine of justification by faith alone. This doctrine was scandalous in the light of the medieval church and its practice of redemption by what Calvin called somewhere "the sacramental treadmill." And when the Reformers began to discover Scripture simply by reading it, they recognized that Scripture was not indifferent to tradition. Rather, Scripture was beginning to judge the traditions of the church. Thus, in the Reformers' view, the traditions of the church, if one was to be loyal to the Scriptures, had to change.

The Roman church was faced with a great problem at this point, because some of the traditions of the church were immensely profitable. For instance, visitors to Rome today who go to St. Peter's Basilica to marvel at all the art and architecture there often have no idea that that beautiful structure was built with the money that came with the indulgences that so outraged Luther. At the time, the traditions of the church, in Luther's judgment, were guilty of enabling the selling of salvation. Certainly, that was the way indulgences functioned in much of the world at the time.

What was the Roman church to do? The Reformers were blowing the whistle on these kinds of practices. And they were doing it on the basis of the very teaching that the Roman church acknowledged. Thus, the Church of Rome convened the Council of Trent to decide, in effect, the best strategy for dealing with the Reformers. What they decided at the Council of Trent regarding the place of tradition in the formal theology of their system was something that was momentous and very unfortunate. The council said that God does not speak merely through his Word but through tradition as well. Trent said that Scripture and tradition are not in a relationship in which one judges the other, but rather, both are on the same level.

The Roman church lifted tradition up and put it on the same level as the Scriptures. They said, in effect, "Well, God speaks in both ways, and therefore we can keep these things because God has obviously spoken through the combined wisdom and counsel of the cardinals and the pope." And of course, we know how such a view of Scripture and tradition has played out in history.

Protestant Problems with Scripture

In the Protestant church, the proper relationship between Scripture and tradition was maintained for a long time. But then, as a result of rationalism and the attacks of modernism on the Bible, Scripture (in the minds of most mainline Protestants, at least) began to lose the unique position that it had had all down through the history of the church. Increasingly, the Bible was not seen as God's Word to man and therefore truthful, trustworthy, and inerrant. Rather, it began to be seen primarily as the word of man about God. The modernists were not (at this point, at least) saying that the Bible was necessarily untruthful. But it was certainly subject to the same kind of error or mixture of truth and error that everything human seems to have. Such was their argument.

What happened at that point is that Scripture, in the mind of the Protestant churches, was brought down from the high place it had occupied all down through the centuries of Christendom to the same level as tradition at the time of the Reformation. But even here, in theory there is a vast difference between the views of the modernists and the views of the Church of Rome. In Rome's teaching, we have two sure words from God: Scripture and the pope's *ex cathedra* teaching. But according to modernism, we have no sure words from God. We simply have human muddlings after God, which may or may not be true.

However much these two views differ in theory, in practice they arrive at much the same place. This is because men and women are sinful, and unless we have the objective standard of the Word of God judging our traditions, we end up preferring them to the Word of God. Thus the Roman church, though it had the two standards, leaned increasingly on its traditions. It had little trouble, then, ultimately departing from what the Word of God clearly says. My point in this discussion is simply to reiterate that we must recover the Reformation doctrine of Scripture. We must do so strongly, intelligently, and articulately in our time.

The Problem of Subjectivism

Not only did the Reformers have to contend with the corrupt traditions of Rome, but they had another problem as well. As the Reformation got underway, and as people began to discover the Word of God, they fell into a kind of subjectivism in some quarters that led to various kinds of excesses. Such excesses were justified on the basis of the alleged leading of the Holy Spirit. People would argue, "Well, we are Spirit-filled men, and the Holy Spirit has told us thus and so. Therefore, that's what we are going to do." And they would do that without any real anchoring in the Word of God.

Now, what the Reformers said at this point was that it was true that the Spirit must work in us for us to understand God's Word. But God's Word just is the Scriptures, and therefore the Spirit works to illuminate the Word. The Bible is the objective base, so to speak, and the Spirit is the One who works to enable us to understand it and apply it to our lives. Whenever the church separates these two, she gets into trouble. Similarly, today we have a kind of subjectivism that is extremely dangerous.

I heard a particularly extreme example of this subjectivism several years ago when I was out on the West Coast. I was in the San Francisco area for a regional meeting of ICBI on a Friday afternoon; the meetings began that night. I was off somewhere driving, so I turned on the radio just to listen and hear what was happening. As I scanned the dial, I was arrested by the sound of church bells—lovely, sonorous church bells. I thought, "Perhaps this is vespers at Grace Cathedral in San Francisco. I'll listen." So I stopped. It wasn't the vespers at all; it was a recording. It was an introduction to a call-in talk show, the catchphrase of which was this: "Have you had a spiritual experience?" The idea was that if you had had a spiritual experience, you were to call the station and recount your experience over the air.

I heard two callers while I was listening. Apparently, one of them was a young woman who had owned a home in the northern part of the state. One day she felt that she should leave home and travel down along the coast. In fact, she felt that she should hitchhike down the coastal road until she got about halfway between San Francisco and Los Angeles. And then she sensed that this was the place, so she asked the driver to stop. She got out of the car and went down the hillside toward the ocean, and she found a cave there.

She went on to explain how she camped out for three days, getting up each day to swim around in the water, mingling with the seaweed and having a kind of spiritual experience. She then explained that about the third day an animal came by and went off in a certain direction. She took this as a sign that it was time to go. So she climbed back up the hillside, she hitchhiked back home, and that was her spiritual experience. That was the first caller.

The second call I heard was even more bizarre. This was apparently an older woman. Now, this was about the time that Jimmy Carter and Ronald Reagan had been running against each other for the presidency. This woman described what had happened to her on election day. She began by saying, "I've been a Democrat all my life, and I went into the polling place fully expecting to vote for Jimmy Carter."

"But," she continued, "when I got inside and they closed the curtain, some strange power came over me, and I don't know why, but I pulled the lever for Ronald Reagan." She didn't say whether she thought that experience was benign or demonic, but since she was a Democrat, I think she was suggesting that it was a demonic experience!

Though this woman's experience is somewhat funny in that context, it is not altogether different from the kind of things one hears in evangelical churches. The question that arises is whether or not this is the way that God really speaks. In other words, does God speak in those subjective, supernatural ways, like the two callers outlined above?

The Reformers said, "No." They would allow that God could order circumstances in a special way. But what they wanted to emphasize was the fact that God speaks in Scripture and that therefore the way to have the leading of God is to come to the Word of God. We come to the Word and then pray and allow the Holy Spirit of God to give our human minds understanding of what we read. Given the illuminating power of the Holy Spirit, we find in the Bible the principles that are necessary for living a godly life.

This reminds me of another story about Luther. After he had translated the Bible into German, and that translation of the Bible became so popular, he was often presented with copies of his own Bible to sign. Luther often used this as an opportunity to preach. When he was given a copy of his Bible to sign, he would write a verse in it and then he would give a little sermon on that verse. Some of these have survived, and I am reminded of one in particular.

Luther wrote on one occasion the verse John 8:25. That verse reads, "So they said to him, 'Who are you?' Jesus said to them, 'Just what I have been telling you from the beginning.'" And then Luther wrote this:

They, that is those who ask the question, desire to know who he is and not to regard what he says, while he desires them first to listen and then they will know who he is. So this is the rule: listen and allow the word to make the beginning. Then the knowing will nicely follow. If, however, you do not listen, you will never know anything. For it is decreed God will not be seen, known, or comprehended except through his word alone. Whatever, therefore, one undertakes for salvation apart from the word, is in vain. God will not respond to that, he will not have it, he will not tolerate any other way. Therefore, let his book, in which he speaks with you, be commended to you, for he did not cause it to be written for no purpose. He did not want us to lie there in neglect as if he were speaking with mice under the bench or with flies on the pulpit. We are to read it, to think and speak about it, and to study it, certain that he himself and not an angel or creature is speaking with us in it.[5]

This understanding of *sola Scriptura* is vastly needed in the church today. If, on the one hand, we want to avoid being taken captive by our traditions and, on the other hand, avoid the excesses that come from an essentially subjective experience (which is the more common error today, I think), there is one thing we must do. We must listen to God speaking in his Word.

What a Strong Commitment to Scripture Will Do for the Church

Shifting gears, we need to look at what a strong commitment to Scripture will do for the church today. As it did during the Reformation, a strong commitment to the highest possible view of Scripture will strengthen the church. It will do so in at least two different ways.

5. Martin Luther, "Only the Bible to Teach about God," in *What Luther Says*, 81.

First, it will make the individual Christian strong. We live in an age of relativism in which, apart from Scripture (sometimes in the church, but certainly in the world), there is no certainty of what truth is. I remember the first time I came across this idea of relativism. I hadn't even been thinking along those lines. I was still thinking that truth was truth and falsehood was falsehood. But I was reading C. S. Lewis's *Screwtape Letters* at the time. In one of the opening letters, the devil Screwtape is advising the junior devil Wormwood about tempting his friend. And in essence, the senior devil tells Wormwood that it was wrong of him to bring an atheist to argue against the man who is thinking of becoming a Christian. This is, argues the devil, because men are no longer persuaded by arguments. That used to be the way, he says, but no longer.[6]

In effect, what Lewis was saying was that people are operating with relativistic assumptions today. They don't really grapple with the question of truth as they used to. Rather, they choose to think that there is no such thing as certainty or truth.

The second and more extensive place I came across this idea was in the writings of Francis Schaeffer. He makes a great deal about relativism (rightly, I think), saying that since the time of G. W. F. Hegel, we have lived, philosophically and practically, in a relativistic world where truth is not truth, at least in a permanent sense. Rather, it is truth only for the moment. Hegel argued that truth comes by way of the ideas of thesis, antithesis, and synthesis.

Essentially, here's what Hegel meant by these terms. He taught that in any particular moment in history, there is a dominant idea that people regard as true and that is the thesis. But because there is no such thing as absolute truth,

6. C. S. Lewis, *The Screwtape Letters* (New York: Macmillan, 1943), 11.

the thesis, inevitably, produces a reaction to it, which is an antithesis. Then those two begin to fight it out in history. And as they fight it out, different parts of each are rubbed off and new ideas emerge and the two come together. When this happens, we arrive at what Hegel called a synthesis. This synthesis becomes the new thesis, which in turn produces another antithesis and another struggle and another synthesis, and so on.

Hegel said that all of history is like that. Interestingly enough (though not surprisingly), Hegel's ideas were taken over into theology and applied to biblical history by a man named Ferdinand Christian Baur. He argued that the history of the early church proceeded according to Hegel's description; there was the theology of Paul and the theology of Peter, and that was the thesis and the antithesis. And then there was a struggle, and out of that came early Catholicism. This is what Baur was arguing.

Most people today do not operate in any philosophically self-conscious way. Therefore, they may not use Hegel's terms, but they practically live out his ideas. If you doubt this, just think of the experiences you may have had in trying to talk about Jesus Christ. A generation ago, if you tried to talk about Christianity and its supernatural aspects, you would talk about things such as the resurrection and the virgin birth. You might also speak of the necessity of Christ's atoning work on the cross and being saved by faith alone in that work.

As I said, a generation ago, if you had talked that way and people did not want to believe it, you'd get an argument. People would say to you, "No, that's not true. We live in a scientific age, and we know today that things like miracles don't happen: dead men don't come to life and virgins don't give birth to children." They might argue that, morally speaking, it is impossible for one person to pay the penalty for the sin of another, and so on. That was the kind of argument you would get.

But if you've talked to anyone about the claims of Christ recently, you know that this situation described above does not happen much anymore. Today, if you talk to people about the Lord, generally what you will hear is something along these lines: "Well, I'm glad you've found something that's meaningful for you. I'm really very happy for you. I'm glad you can believe that, but that's really just not my bag." What they're saying, you see, is that truth is relative. They're saying, "That's your truth, but just because it's your truth doesn't mean it's my truth. It doesn't have to be my truth; I'll find truth of my own. And just because it's true today even for you doesn't mean, necessarily, that it's going to be true tomorrow." So truth changes, in history, and truth varies from person to person.

One of the many glaring problems with this Hegelian view is, of course, that when we cut ourselves off from any idea of absolute truth, ultimate meaning and ultimate responsibility disappear along with absolute truth. If we don't have a sure word from God, we don't have a measuring stick, so to speak, for anything. If we don't have a measuring stick for anything, then ultimately what we do doesn't matter at all. And one place where this kind of relativism shows itself clearly today is in the area of language.

The Wretched Effects of Relativism

Some years ago, I was told about an incident that happened in one of our liberal seminaries. One of the professors was talking about the function of language, and he was making the point that language was not an absolute, so to speak. It does not even point to absolute things. Language is a subjective enterprise, he reasoned, and what it means to you is not necessarily what it means to me. So a word doesn't carry any positive content.

Rightly, the students were objecting to this teaching. They were arguing, "Well, it is true that sometimes words are ambiguous, and it is true that if I use a word, you don't necessarily understand what I mean. But that's what theology is all about— trying to clarify words and communicate well."

Basically, these students were saying that the reason we can communicate is that all language is based on God. The gift of language is something that he has given to us. We are made in his image. Therefore, we have that absolute, which we don't always attain. But the fact that the absolute is there is what makes the language meaningful. That's what the students were saying to this professor.

Well, the professor wasn't buying this at all. One of the students even used an illustration. He said that if he were to look out the window and say, "Look! An airplane!" then people would look up in the sky and not on the ground. Why? For the simple reason that everyone there knew what an airplane was and where to look for it.

Still, the professor was not buying it. And the argument wasn't going anywhere until one of the students said, "Well, you know, if language doesn't have any real meaning, then our being here, talking about language, doesn't have any real meaning." And that sank in. And someone else said, "Are you saying, then, that our being here is meaningless?" And the other student said, "Yes, that is what follows." "Well," they said, "if our being here is meaningless, what are we going to do for the rest of the hour?" And one of the students who had been sitting in the back, probably not paying much attention anyway, said, "Let's go out and play squash." So the whole class got up and walked out the door, and they left the professor there with his theory.

Something similar happens theologically as well. In effect, this is what is happening in many of our churches. We're not saying anything that has any real effect on people because so often what we're saying is not based on the Word of God. And people, whether they approach it philosophically or not, realize that something is missing. They realize that what they are hearing is ultimately meaningless, and so they are voting the same way the students did—with their feet. They are leaving the churches that do not offer them anything different from the world and its theories.

So a high view of the Bible and a strong commitment to the Word of God will strengthen the individual Christian against the seeming tidal wave of relativism that is sweeping across our culture. In fact, the view of the Bible that the Reformers held is the only thing that can stem such a tide for the individual believer.

A Strong Commitment to the Word of God in Preaching

The second area in which we need this strength for the church is in the area of preaching. I have spent a lot of time in ecclesiastical circles where there is a considerable amount of unbelief. In my experience, there is far more unbelief among the clergy than the laymen ever suspect. And the reason for that, of course, is that if most preachers said what they really believed or failed to believe, they'd lose their jobs. So they don't say what they really believe, and they pretend to believe certain truths of Christianity. They lack the conviction that

Luther and Calvin and the other Reformers had about the truths of Scripture. To be sure, these subtle unbelievers will say what they believe in their own circles, but never in front of laypeople.

I was at a meeting once where there were a great many professors and pastors; it was sort of a strategy session for the denomination. And I had been given the opportunity of representing the evangelical point of view, so I did just that. I thought I was rather wise in doing it. I tried to use language that would not offend. And I was certainly doing everything I could to win them over to my side. So I spoke about the "historical Jesus"—a good theological term with a whole century of German criticism behind it. And I thought to myself, "Maybe this is the way to go." I spoke of people being lost; I used a lot of scriptural texts to explain what that meant.

When I got to the end, a professor from one of the seminaries stood up in the back and said, "Don't you understand that there's no such thing as the historical Jesus?" "Well, as a matter of fact," I answered, "I had not. I kind of thought there was." And he said, "Don't you know that every one of the Gospels was written to contradict the other Gospels?" Well, I hadn't been aware of that, either. I had been studying the Gospels, and I thought that the idea in all four was a complementary picture of Jesus Christ. "No," he said, "every one was written to contradict the others."

And then, because I had spoken in an unguarded moment of the return of Jesus Christ, he said, "We have got to get it into our heads that Jesus Christ is never coming back and all things are going to continue as they have from the beginning." Well, when he said that, I was surprised. Perhaps unknown to him, he was actually quoting from one of the letters of the apostle Peter, who urged his readers to remember God's Word,

[for] scoffers will come in the last days with scoffing, following their own sinful desires. They will say, "Where is the promise of his coming? For ever since the fathers fell asleep, all things are continuing as they were from the beginning of creation." (2 Peter 3:3–4)

Heresy, you know, is that which, if you believe it, prevents you from continuing to be a Christian. Now, this professor had gone on to say that believing the Bible was equivalent to heresy. So to believe the Bible is to believe that which disqualifies you from the Christian faith. Here's how he put it: "To invest the Bible with the qualities of inerrancy and infallibility is to idolatrize [*sic*] it, to transform it into a false god." Now, this is a false idea in and of itself, but it is, I'm afraid, a majority report among many a clergyman and professor. He went on to dismissively label a high view of Scripture as "simplistic."

We're told at this point that the reason for this great change in the thinking of the pastors and the professors in many of the churches is that the latest evidence has simply made it impossible to have that high but simplistic view of the Bible that the Reformers and others before us in the history of the church have had. This is what I was told in seminary, and I particularly wrestled with this problem. Was it true, I asked, that as the data has come in from history, linguistic studies, the study of comparative religions, archaeology, and all those things that fit into a study of the New Testament and Old Testament, the historical reliability of the Bible has suffered? Well, what I discovered was that this particular idea was itself wrong.

On the contrary, as the data has come in over the last decades, the historical reliability of the Bible has been strengthened. It doesn't mean that we understand every single thing we read. It doesn't mean that all the apparent problems have been resolved.

71

But as the data comes in, the tendency is to resolve the problems, not to create more.

Now, we need to proclaim with as much clarity as possible today, because if preaching is to be blessed by God, the men who preach the Bible must be firmly convinced that it is the very Word of God, without error. As I said above, we will probably never solve all the apparent difficulties. But we do have a reliable book in the Bible—a book on which we, as church members and preachers, can stand.

I want to close with a brief quotation from a bishop of the Church of England, J.C. Ryle. He was one of the great evangelical bishops of that church in the nineteenth century, when the scientific criticism was just coming on the scene and affecting many a person's faith. Ryle gave us the Christian attitude toward the Bible and biblical criticism when he wrote, "Give me the 'plenary verbal' theory, with all its difficulties, rather than [doubt]. I accept the difficulties of that theory, and humbly wait for their solution. But while I wait, I feel that I am standing on a rock."[7]

7. J. C. Ryle, *Expository Thoughts on the Gospels: For Family and Private Use*, vol. 1 (New York: Robert Carter & Brothers, 1879), vii.

5

God's Mighty Word

RICHARD D. PHILLIPS

For as the rain and the snow come down from heaven and do not return there but water the earth, making it bring forth and sprout, giving seed to the sower and bread to the eater, so shall my word be that goes out from my mouth; it shall not return to me empty, but it shall accomplish that which I purpose, and shall succeed in the thing for which I sent it. (Isaiah 55:10–11)

ON THE OCCASION of his twenty-fifth anniversary in the pulpit of Philadelphia's Tenth Presbyterian Church, in 1952, Donald Grey Barnhouse gave an address titled "Holding Forth the Word." In that address, he told a story from his earliest days as pastor. Just a week or two after he had been installed as minister, he entered the pulpit, which in those days had a great pulpit Bible resting on it. Barnhouse opened it randomly, placing his own Bible and sermon notes upon its pages. Looking down, he realized that he had turned to a passage recording a curse upon the nations. Wanting something a bit more encouraging for his preaching, he looked for a passage that would set forth a great promise from God. He quickly made his decision, turning in that Bible to Isaiah chapter 55, which contains this well-known passage:

> For as the rain and the snow come down from heaven
> > and do not return there but water the earth,
> making it bring forth and sprout,
> > giving seed to the sower and bread to the eater,
> so shall my word be that goes out from my mouth;
> > it shall not return to me empty,
> but it shall accomplish that which I purpose,
> > and shall succeed in the thing for which I sent it.

To Barnhouse's surprise, he discovered that his predecessors had apparently done the same thing, because the page of the pulpit Bible was worn on that text. He later commented that the pages containing the great fifty-fifth chapter of Isaiah, and the preceding page with the fifty-third chapter of Isaiah concerning the Lord Jesus Christ as God's Lamb, give mute evidence that the men who had stood in the pulpit of Tenth Church for more than a century were men of the living Word and the written Word.[1]

Barnhouse was impressed by what this said about the convictions of the men who had stood in that pulpit before him; they were the same convictions with which he himself ministered. They were persuaded that the Bible as the very Word of God is the foundation

---

1. Donald Grey Barnhouse, "Isaiah 55:11," in *Holding Forth the Word: 1927–1952*, Manuscript Collection of Tenth Presbyterian Church, Philadelphia.

of any faithful and effective gospel ministry. Barnhouse therefore concluded his anniversary service by offering this prayer:

> It is my prayer that no man shall ever stand in this pulpit as long as time shall last who does not desire to have all that he does based upon this Book. For this Book does not *contain* the Word of God, it *is* the Word of God. And though we may preach the Word with all the stammering limitations of our human nature, the grace of God does the miracle of the ministry, and through human lips speaks the divine Word, and the hearts of the people are refreshed.[2]

God's Revealed Word

Barnhouse prayed that way because he believed what the Bible says about itself. He had experienced the power of God's mighty Word in his own life and ministry. This is a hallmark of a true servant of God. He is a man who has resolved not only to believe, but also to rely on what God has set forth in his Word. The prophet Isaiah was such a man. And in the fifty-fifth chapter of his prophecy, God speaks through him to declare the reasons why God's people may place their hope on that which comes from God's holy Word.

The first reason we may rely on the Bible is that it *is God's revealed Word*. The Bible is God's own revelation to mankind, containing, as the Westminster Confession of Faith puts it, "the whole counsel of God concerning all things necessary for His own glory, man's salvation, faith and life" (1.6).

There are those who hold that the Bible consists merely of the inspired thoughts of men in their own spiritual quest or, as

2. Ibid.

others put it, that the Bible contains the history of a particular religious experience or tradition. We certainly admit human authorship of the books that make up the Bible. But we do not find a single writer who says that what he wrote is his own attempt to understand God or come to grips with the eternal. Not one of them says, "I have been wrestling with these ideas, and I want to share them with you." What they say is this: "The Word of the Lord came to me." Specifically, Isaiah is essentially claiming that, just as rain and snow come down from heaven, the word of God came down from heaven to earth, so to speak. God describes the Scriptures as "my word . . . that goes out from my mouth" (Isa. 55:11). This means that the Bible does not *become* the Word of God as we find our thoughts inspired by it. The Bible *is* the Word of God because it comes from God as he speaks from heaven to the barren hearts of men on earth.

A New Testament verse that strongly aligns with Isaiah 55:10–11 is 2 Timothy 3:16. Paul was advising Timothy on how to succeed in ministry amid all kinds of trials. He encouraged Timothy to put his trust in the Scriptures. Why? Because "all Scripture is breathed out by God." Paul identifies the Bible as the very Word of God that Isaiah spoke about, the Word that goes forth from his mouth and comes down from heaven.

We speak of the Bible as being *inspired*, but more accurately, the Bible speaks of itself as being *expired*—out-breathed from the very mouth of God, a true and genuine revelation directly from God to us through the human writers. Yes, God used human agents, but the Scriptures do not have their origin in the experience or the ideas or the will of the human writers. Peter explained, "For no prophecy was ever produced by the will of man, but men spoke from God as they were carried along by the Holy Spirit" (2 Peter 1:21).

It is necessary for us that God should have revealed himself, for otherwise we could never know the most important things about life and eternity. There are some things that we can know about God simply from the created order. Paul writes, "His invisible attributes, namely, his eternal power and divine nature, have been clearly perceived, ever since the creation of the world, in the things that have been made" (Rom. 1:20). But beyond that, man naturally wonders what God is like. What does God intend for us, and what does God demand from us? Apart from God's revealed Word, there is no way for us to know these things. This shows how necessary the Bible is for every Christian, and why it is the duty of the church to teach and preach what God has revealed in his Word.

Henry Augustus Boardman, one of Barnhouse's predecessors at Tenth Presbyterian Church, put it this way:

> Shut up your Bible, and what do you know of that [spiritual] world? What do you know of God, of yourself, of retribution, of the possibility of forgiveness? . . . What does conscience, or reason, or the light of nature, reveal concerning the pardon of sin and future happiness? Nothing—literally nothing. The insatiate craving of the soul for information on this vital question is met only by guesses and conjectures, baseless, illusive, without authority, and, therefore, without consolation.[3]

This is what God says in the verses that precede the verses we are studying:

> For my thoughts are not your thoughts,
>   neither are your ways my ways, declares the LORD.
> For as the heavens are higher than the earth,
>   so are my ways higher than your ways
>   and my thoughts than your thoughts. (Isa. 55:8–9)

3. Henry Augustus Boardman, "A Brief Plea with the Infidel," *The Presbyterian Magazine*, vol. 6, ed. C. Van Rensselaer (Philadelphia: Joseph M. Wilson, 1856), 157.

This is why it is especially the gospel of Jesus Christ that is beyond human comprehension, except as it is taught from the Bible. The idea that God's holy Son should die an atoning death for our sins and that we should be justified through faith alone proceeds from a higher wisdom than we have encountered before. We all need to hear the gospel regularly, precisely because our native ways take us in a different direction—the direction of flesh, of pride, of human strength and boasting—and away from God's one way of salvation. Therefore, not only must the preacher teach the Word of God, but the whole congregation must resolve to be taught of God as the Bible is expounded.

And this is why this text has so shaped my own pastoral ministry. My thinking is shaped by the Westminster Confession of Faith, which differs from all prior Reformed confessions in that it begins not with a statement of the nature of God or of the gospel itself, but with a chapter on the nature and authority of the Holy Scriptures. The reason the framers of the confession opted to begin with a statement about Scripture is that we must first understand where our ideas about God and salvation come from. Should preachers preach their own thoughts and ideas, or are they merely to pass on a particular tradition? The Westminster divines clearly expressed their conviction not only that the Bible is God's revealed Word, but that, as such, the Word of God is "most necessary" for God's people (WCF 1.1).

God's Life-Giving Word

So the first reason we must stand upon the Bible is that it is God's revealed Word. But Isaiah gives a second reason, describing the function that God has given his Word: it *brings spiritual blessing to the earth*. Isaiah 55:10 states that God's Word comes to us in the way that rain comes down from heaven onto the earth. God gives us his Word for the purpose that we should come to life and grow spiritually. Without rain the ground becomes hard and lifeless. Similarly, without God's Word we become hard, dry, and dead. Where rain comes, life abounds. The ground becomes green and fruitful as good things come to life.

This idea of the Word of God as rain would have made a strong impression on the original readers of Isaiah's prophecy. One commentator explains it this way:

> In the ancient Near East rain spelled the difference between life and death. If the rains came at the appropriate times one could hope for good crops, which meant enough food (bread) for the coming year, and, of at least equal importance, *seed* for the following year's crop. If the rains did not come, not only was the crop lost but also the seed, and famine stared one in the face. In a powerful comparison, Isaiah says that God's word is just like the rain. . . . [It] achieves the purposes of blessing and life-giving for which it was intended.[4]

Things are not much different today. When flying in an airplane high above the ground, I like to look down over portions of the country that are arid and bare. All will be brown or gray in every direction, but then I will spy a line of bright green. What is it that I see? It is water! Where there is water, there is life. And God's Word comes down to our dry souls as the rain falls on barren land, bringing things to life and giving blessing to needy souls. Therefore, the only way for us to be strong in faith and to abound in life is to eat and drink from the Word of the Lord.

This teaching finds strong support in the New Testament. We think of Jesus' willingly enduring a lengthy fast in the desert

4. John Oswalt, *Isaiah 40–66* (Grand Rapids: Eerdmans, 1998), 446.

as the devil tempted him, sustained not by physical bread but by the Word of God. "Man shall not live by bread alone," he told the devil, "but by every word that comes from the mouth of God" (Matt. 4:4, quoting Deut. 8:3). Likewise, when Jesus was departing from this world, he prayed for his disciples: "Sanctify them in the truth; your word is truth" (John 17:17).

But one of the passages that most dramatically illustrates this truth is found in the Old Testament prophet Ezekiel. Ezekiel lived in a time of great spiritual decline; his days saw the deportation of many Jews into the Babylonian captivity and ultimately the destruction of Jerusalem because of unbelief and sin. What was a prophet to do in such times? The answer that God gave Ezekiel was the same answer that Paul gave to young Timothy. The Lord brought him down in the middle of a valley that was full of bones. The prophet recounts: "He led me around among them, and behold, there were very many on the surface of the valley, and behold, they were very dry" (Ezek. 37:2). The site before him was sickening and grotesque: dry, bleached human bones, scattered around a wretched valley of death. It was, of course, a picture of the spiritual context in which Ezekiel was called to minister.

The question is often raised as to what we should do to renew spiritual interest in our generation. How are we going to reach people who are disinterested in God and salvation, who (spiritually speaking) are not only dry, but dead? If what we desire is attracting them to the programs and services of the church, then we will market worldly goods to them. If we are appealing to the flesh, we will talk about things that are interesting to them. Such an approach is what most of the church-growth seminars advise today. But if we are interested in helping people to come to real spiritual life, if we desire that their souls would no longer be entombed in the hard rock of unbelief and sin, then we will employ the kind of supernatural means that only God can supply.

This is what God taught Ezekiel. He asked, "Son of man, can these bones live?" (Ezek. 37:3). That is a question for our own times! I have always loved Ezekiel's answer: "O Lord GOD, you know" (37:3). So God answered him: "Prophesy over these bones, and say to them, O dry bones, hear the word of the LORD" (37:4). God meant, "Preach! Preach the Word of the Lord, preacher!" So Ezekiel began preaching, and as he did the most astonishing things began to happen. "As I prophesied," he wrote, "there was a sound, and behold, a rattling, and the bones came together, bone to its bone. And I looked, and behold, there were sinews on them, and flesh had come upon them, and skin had covered them" (37:7–8). Then God called down his Spirit upon the dead bodies, and Ezekiel marveled: "The breath came into them, and they lived and stood on their feet, an exceedingly great army" (37:10).

This is exactly how true ministry works. People's lives are unwhole and disintegrated. Their values and beliefs do not fit together with the real needs of their lives. They are like a skeleton whose bones have been scattered. But as they are exposed to the preached Word, things begin to come together and over time things that were confusing start to make sense. And at the time of God's choosing, new life is breathed from on high into their souls. They live. They stand for Christ. They form together as a spiritual militia, and in time they are trained as an army for the Lord. This is precisely what our generation needs: a Christian church that is strong and well armed with truth and the fruits of God's Word, and that goes forth into the world on the divine mission of salvation. But how will this happen—especially in our times, which seem so similar to Ezekiel's? God answers, "Prophesy! Preach!" As we do God's work in God's way, with

God's power, the sovereign Lord declares: "I will put my Spirit within you, and you shall live, and I will place you in your own land. Then you shall know that I am the LORD; I have spoken, and I will do it, declares the LORD" (Ezek. 37:14).

We are living in a generation in which the church has little confidence in the preached Word. Preaching is insufficient to meet modern needs, we are continually told. Moreover, we are instructed to harness the insights of sociology and psychology. We must marry ourselves with the harlot-wife of Hollywood and heed the jaded counsel of Madison Avenue advertisers. Yet salvation always is and always will be a divine work of sovereign grace. What we need, what our generation requires, is life from above. And as Peter said: "You have been born again, not of perishable seed but of imperishable, through the living and abiding word of God" (1 Peter 1:23). God has placed into our hands his mightiest weapon for saving power: the life-giving water of his Word. He promises, "For as the rain and the snow come down from heaven and do not return there but water the earth, making it bring forth and sprout, giving seed to the sower and bread to the eater, so shall my word be that goes out from my mouth" (Isa. 55:10–11).

God's Effectual Word

So God's Word is necessary and essential and central to the life and work of the church because it is God's own revelation to man and the life-giving rain that falls down from heaven. But in Isaiah 55:11, God gives us an even greater reason to take our stand on his Word. He says that it *is effectual in achieving what God has purposed for it*. Not only is the Bible a revealed Word from heaven and a nourishing Word for those on the earth, but it is a mighty Word that, God says, "shall not return to me empty, but it shall accomplish that which I purpose, and shall succeed in the thing for which I sent it."

The reason it is mighty, of course, is that it is God's Word; it is not like the word of man. Martin Luther made the difference plain: "We must make a great difference between God's Word and the word of man. A man's word is a little sound, that flies into the air, and soon vanishes; but the Word of God is greater than heaven and earth, yea, greater than death and hell, for it forms part of the power of God, and endures everlastingly."[5] As was true in the days of creation, when God spoke and there was light, God's Word carries with it God's power. It is completely effective in achieving God's purpose, either for salvation or for judgment.

All these things may also be said about the Lord Jesus Christ, who is the living Word. Jesus was sent to earth from heaven as the most complete revelation from God. He came to bring life and abundance, delivering us from our sins. Furthermore, his saving work on the cross is wholly effectual for all his own, fully accomplishing God's purpose of salvation for the elect. He is the living Word who is brought to us by the written Word. And God has appointed that Word of Christ to be the sole instrument by which sinners are converted and saved and made strong in their faith. The Word of Christ is the way that he is glorified in the life and work of his church here on earth.

We are saved by faith alone in Christ alone. From where, then, does faith come? The Bible says, "Faith comes from hearing, and hearing through the word of Christ" (Rom. 10:17). And of this faith, based on and born of his own Word, Christ gives his

5. Martin Luther, *That Doctrines of Men Are to Be Rejected*; quoted in James Montgomery Boice, *Foundations of the Christian Faith* (Downers Grove, IL: IVP Academic, 1986), 69.

promise: "On this rock I will build my church, and the gates of hell shall not prevail against it" (Matt. 16:18).

A Closing Prayer

I began this chapter by recalling the notable prayer of Donald Grey Barnhouse as he asked the Lord to ensure that his successors would be like-minded men in relying on the power of God's mighty Word. I have the privilege not only of being inspired by Barnhouse's prayer, but also of being a direct beneficiary of that prayer. For that very pulpit was the nursery in which my own ministry was nurtured. It was on that very prayer-soaked granite that I first set my own Bible to preach.

And I pray to God that through the preaching of his Word, God might pour out the waters of life upon needy souls in our own day, so that households may receive and grow in the salvation that he alone gives. I long to see many saved, and that God may receive the glory he deserves in faithful pulpits across our land and throughout the world. Indeed, we should pray that God would grant that all who preach until the return of Christ will be men who stand upon the Word of God and faithfully hold it forth in the power of the Holy Spirit. May preachers be those who rely on the life-giving power that proceeds only from God's mighty Word.

6

The Word in the Church

MARK DEVER

Then he said to me, "Prophesy over these bones, and
say to them, O dry bones, hear the word of the LORD."
(Ezek. 37:4)

THERE ARE THREE basic needs that the church has
always had and has sharply today. First, the church needs to
have the Word of God at the center—not at the periphery—of
its mission. Second, the church needs to have the real gospel,
not a false one. Third, the church needs to be distinct from the
world, not lost in it.

In this chapter, I want to focus on the first of these.
While the other two are not unimportant, given the nature
of this book, we will focus mainly on the place of the Word
in the church today.

The Word of God at the Center

Today, a lot is written about the church that does not at all have the Word at the center. In fact, the Word is quite peripheral. I spend a fair amount of time reading books on what makes a really good church. I find that the answers range from everything from the friendliness of the people in the church, to how effective the prospective church is in its financial planning, to being sensitive to people, to having vibrant music, to having pleasant surroundings, to having pristine bathrooms and plentiful parking, to having exciting children's programs, to having elaborate Sunday school options, and so forth. And these are being peddled to Christians and to church leaders and pastors as *the key* to helping a church grow and become "the best."

The question I want to pose is simple: "What do you think makes a church healthy?" If statistics indicate anything, you're going to be moving in the next few years. You'll have to look for a church in the community to which you move. How do you evaluate that church? If you're a member of your own local church and you're in any kind of leadership position, or you simply talk to other people in the church, you want to know what makes up a healthy church.

We all need to know what makes a church healthy because of the various answers to this question the experts give today. Many of them will tell you that it's everything from how religion-free your language is to how invisible your membership requirements are. Are secure nurseries and sparkling bathrooms really the way to church growth, health, and revival?

Topical or Expository?

I think the first and primary mark of a healthy church is the centrality of the Word in the church, particularly as it is expressed in expository preaching. Now, really, this is far and away the most important mark of a healthy church. I'm convinced that if you get this one right, others will follow. That is, if you miss this one but maybe you get some of the other things that we will cover later, then those will eventually be discarded or distorted because they didn't spring from the Word in the first place. But if you get the priority of the Word established, then you have the single most important aspect of the church's life in place. And with that the growing health of the church is virtually assured, whatever happens numerically.

So what is this all-important thing called expository preaching? It is usually set in contrast to topical preaching. Topical preaching is when a certain topic in the Bible is selected and taught, in contrast to taking a text of the Bible and preaching it. The topical sermon begins with a particular topic that the preacher wants to preach about, and then he finds that truth reflected in a particular passage or maybe several texts in Scripture. Stories and anecdotes are combined, and all are woven together around one theme.

Now, a topical sermon can certainly be expositional, insofar as it uses texts carefully and well. But the point of the sermon in a topical sermon was already determined before the preacher ever came to the Word. The point of the sermon was determined by his own thought of what it was that the congregation needed to hear.

Again, this kind of preaching is contrasted with how I usually preach on the Lord's Day at my church in Washington. There I preach expository sermons. I approach a text of Scripture and it determines what I will say. The text determines what my points are going to be and what things I am going to say to God's people on any given Lord's Day.

Expository preaching is not simply preaching a verse-by-verse commentary orally from the pulpit. Such teaching can sometimes be preaching. But expository preaching is certainly not only that. Rather, expository preaching is preaching that takes the main point of the sermon from the main point of the biblical text that is being expounded.

Expository preaching is preaching in service to the Word. It presumes a belief in the authority of Scripture, but it is something more than that. This is because a commitment to expositional preaching is a commitment to hear God's Word. It arises out of affection for God and a desire to hear from him. It comes from a realization that spiritual life and growth comes through hearing God's Word. Preaching, then, that is expositional (or *expository*; they mean the same thing) is God's Word being brought to God's people.

The Old Testament prophets and New Testament apostles were not just given a commission to go and speak, but they were given a particular message to deliver. Thus, I don't really believe it when Christian preachers come to me and say that they are called to preach. Sadly, when I listen to them, sometimes I think that's all they think they were called to do.

Let me explain. I think that if a man is really called to preach in a truly Christian sense, he is not merely called to preach. He is not merely called to speak. He is called to preach God's Word. He is called to speak God's message. And if he is not preaching God's Word or speaking his message, then he is not truly called to preach. I don't care what subjective experiences of "guidance" are brought forward—I think if someone is not preaching God's Word, he is wrong. God's ministers are called to be just that: servants of God's Word. That's what we are to give to his people. And insofar as we do not spend ourselves in giving that Word to God's people, we are not true ministers. We are not true preachers.

Christian preachers today have authority to speak from God only so long as they speak his words. Preachers are not simply commanded to preach. They are commanded specifically to preach *the Word*. Now, pastors may happily accept the authority of God's Word. They may even profess to believe in the inerrancy of the Bible.

If a preacher professes to believe in the authority and inerrancy of God's Word and does not regularly preach expositionally, then one finds that he doesn't preach any more than he already knew when he began. For example, he looks for some text somewhere on tithing. Or he gets upset over a lack of modesty in the culture. Or he sees some other true things. He then goes and looks for something in Scripture that will reinforce those ideas and explain and illustrate them.

Topical preaching, then, can take a piece of Scripture and exhort the congregation on a topic that is important without really preaching the point of the passage. It would almost be as though you picked up your Bible, closed your eyes, prayed for guidance, and randomly put your finger on the page. When you open your eyes and read the verse before you, it may bring great blessing to you. But you haven't necessarily learned what God intended to say through that passage understood in its context.

So what is true in real estate is also true in understanding the Bible. The three most important features of real estate (or Scripture interpretation) are location, location, location. The Bible is not like those promise verses in the plastic loaves of bread, written a verse at a time. The Bible was written in books, and we must understand it in context.

Therefore, we don't just take a certain phrase that inspires us and talk about it if we are to be faithful teachers of God's Word. No, we study a particular book and we do our best to understand what's going on in any particular book of the Bible by the Holy Spirit's help. And then a preacher preaches from a particular passage or portion (and that can be as little as one word or phrase or as much as a whole chapter). We take that portion of God's Word and ask, "What is the point of that? Why is that there? What is it saying?" And we bring that, then, to God's people. That's what we want to find at the center of our churches.

I want to repeat this point: someone may happily accept the authority of God's Word and even profess to believe in the inerrancy of the Bible. Yet if that person in practice (whether intended or not) does not preach expositionally, he'll never preach more than he already knows. And from the initial call, to repentance of sins, to the very last thing the Holy Spirit has convicted you about, our whole salvation consists in hearing God in ways in which, before we heard him, we would never have guessed. This is because we are fallen. God must arrest us in our unbelief and disobedience. To charge someone with the responsibility of spiritual oversight of the flock who does not in practice show a commitment to hear and to teach God's Word is to hamper the growth of the church. And practically, this encourages it to grow only to the level of the pastor, so the church will slowly be conformed to the preacher's mind, rather than to God's mind.

Let me quickly add that I do think there are completely legitimate occasions for doing topical teaching, even in the main weekly gathering of the church. But I think the driving force behind the conviction that preaching should normally be expositional is that preaching should have the Word of God at its center. In fact, each and every church should have the Word at its center and should have the Word directing it. And this is because when we read the Scriptures, we see clearly that God has decided to use his Word to bring life. His Word is his own chosen instrument for such an amazing thing.

The Word Creates God's People

I've often recounted the experience I once had at a think-tank meeting in Washington. I was standing around at a reception after somebody had given a lecture on William Tyndale. Well, the fellow giving the lecture had just written a review on a Tyndale biography, as had I. So we found out that we had both just read and responded to this book. And I said, "Well, what did you think of it?" And he said, "Oh, it's a good book, a very good book, except, you know, it had that typical Protestant squint." My friend was a Roman Catholic. And I said, "Really? What's that?" He said, "Well, it is the idea—really the myth—that the Bible created the church when we all know that the church created the Bible."

Well, what was I to do? My friend was being sort of delightfully obnoxious in what he had just said because he knows me and what I believe. So I thought to myself, "I don't really care if he invites me back; I'll just respond."

So I said, "That's ridiculous. God's people have never 'made' God's Word. God's Word has always created God's people. That's the way it's always been. From Genesis 1, when God speaks and the worlds are made; to Genesis 2 and 3, where he speaks and makes man; to Genesis 12, where his word of promise goes out to Abraham and he calls him forth and he makes them his people; to Exodus 3 and 4; from Exodus 20, with the Ten Commandments, where God calls his people out from Egypt; to the examples throughout the history of Israel, like the Word coming to Elijah or coming to Ezekiel;

to, of course, John 1, where the Word comes and takes on flesh. And we find in Romans 10 that faith comes by hearing the message of Christ. God's people have never made God's Word. The pattern is just the reverse: God's Word creates his people." And I really did say all that!

Now, I do not remember what my friend said; he's very urbane. I'm sure he just changed the topic. But it's funny that God used that little conversation with him to really help clarify in my mind that we are not simply dealing with a preference between different kinds of preaching. Expositional preaching is actually God's plan. This is because God creates his people by his Word. So any idea we have of a church where God's Word is not central—well, it's not God's idea. It's not the way he has traditionally worked. It's not the way we see him working in Scripture. God has always created his people by his Word.

I think it might be helpful now if we look through the Bible at some of these things I mentioned to my friend. I want you to be deeply convinced that God's Word creates God's people, not because you take my word for it, but because your eyes have actually looked on the page and seen in God's Word that this is, in fact, the way that God works.

A Survey of God's Creating Word

Let's start where the Bible starts, at Genesis 1. There, we read this phrase again and again: "And God said." It was by his Word that God created the world and all life in it. He spoke and it was so. In chapter 3, of course, we read of the fall. And you see how significant the fall is because our first parents were cast out of the presence of God. They lost sight of God. But by God's grace they did not lose all hope, because though God had banished them from his sight, he mercifully spoke to them. So although they could no longer see him because of their sin, they could hear him speak. This word was their germ of hope: "I will put enmity between you and the woman, and between your offspring and her offspring; he shall bruise your head, and you shall bruise his heel" (Gen. 3:15).

In Genesis 12, we read that it was by God's Word that Abram was called out of Ur of the Chaldees. Again we see that God's people are created by God's Word: "Now the LORD said to Abram, 'Go from your country and your kindred and your father's house to the land that I will show you. And I will make of you a great nation, and I will bless you and make your name great, so that you will be a blessing'" (Gen. 12:1–2). Abram never set up a committee to draft God's Word. He did not go look for the most respectable religious leaders around and try to pool their opinions. No, Abram was made father of God's people because God spoke specially to him. God's Word came and established Abraham's identity in God.

We see the same pattern in the book of Exodus. In Exodus 3:4, God calls out to Moses from the burning bush. So Moses was called by God's Word—again, God uses his Word to call his people to himself. And God's Word came not just to Moses and his descendants, but also to the whole nation of Israel.

Think of Exodus 20, the famous chapter where the Ten Commandments are given by the Lord through Moses. Here again, we read about God speaking to his people, giving his law to them. By their acceptance of it, they were made his people. Exodus 20 recounts a kind of wedding ceremony. This is because it was by God's Word that Israel was constituted God's special people.

And as we keep going through the Old Testament, we see God's Word playing this kind of pivotal role in the lives of his people. Think of that great story of Elijah in 1 Kings 18. How does this chapter begin? "After many days the word of the LORD came to Elijah" (v. 1). How many hundreds of times do we read that phrase in the Old Testament? "The word of the LORD came" to such and such. It is typical of God's activity in the Old Testament, as he created his people by his Word.

God's Word always came as the means of faith in the Old Testament. You can even say that in a secondary sense it was the object of their faith. Now, primarily, God is always the *object* of our faith. But in another sense, his spoken Word is also the *means* of our faith. His promise is to be trusted and relied on with all the faith that we would invest in his person. So his Word is his ambassador to us, as it were. We see, then, in the Old Testament that it was by his Word that God led his people.

Now do you see why the Word of God is so central? God creates his people (and all things) by his Word. He draws them to himself. He creates and re-creates them by his Word. Why is the Word the instrument of creating faith? Because the Word of the Lord is held out to us as the object of our faith. It presents God's promises to us, from all kinds of individual promises in the Old and New Testaments, all the way up to the great promise, the great hope, the great object of our faith—the Word of God incarnate, Christ himself. The Word presents that which is to be believed. To put it another way, it's almost as if, for the Christian, the speed of sound is greater than the speed of light. In other words, we can "hear the future"—it reaches our ears before it reaches our eyes in the Word of God!

From Ezekiel to Jesus

Of course, one of the climactic chapters of the Bible that shows the necessity of the Word imparting life is Ezekiel 37. There, beginning in verse 1, we read:

> The hand of the LORD was upon me, and he brought me out in the Spirit of the LORD and set me down in the middle of the valley; it was full of bones. And he led me around among them, and behold, there were very many on the surface of the valley, and behold, they were very dry. And he said to me, "Son of man, can these bones live?" And I answered, "O Lord GOD, you know." Then he said to me, "Prophesy over these bones, and say to them, O dry bones, hear the word of the LORD. Thus says the Lord GOD to these bones: Behold, I will cause breath to enter you, and you shall live. And I will lay sinews upon you, and will cause flesh to come upon you, and cover you with skin, and put breath in you, and you shall live, and you shall know that I am the LORD."
>
> So I prophesied as I was commanded. And as I prophesied, there was a sound, and behold, a rattling, and the bones came together, bone to its bone. And I looked, and behold, there were sinews on them, and flesh had come upon them, and skin had covered them. But there was no breath in them. Then he said to me, "Prophesy to the breath; prophesy, son of man, and say to the breath, Thus says the Lord GOD: Come from the four winds, O breath, and breathe on these slain, that they may live." So I prophesied as he commanded me, and the breath came into them, and they lived and stood on their feet, an exceedingly great army. (Ezek. 37:1–10)

And then in verse 11 God interprets this vision for Ezekiel. He says that these bones stand for the whole house of Israel, who said, essentially, "Our hope is gone." What a moving presentation this is! This is just a tremendous passage. The hopelessness and the despair of God's people are depicted by this valley full of bones. And it is not just bones. As Ezekiel points out, they are *dry* bones. By highlighting this, God would have us see that these bones have been there a long time. Such a description points to the utter hopelessness of the situation. And here, God's word to his people, as it was to the dry bones in this vision, was: "I will put my Spirit within you, and you shall live" (see Ezek. 37:11–14). Again, how does God do this? By his Word.

Now, in this vision, he does not do what we would do, given a similar opportunity. We would first make an army alive so that they would listen to the prophecy or to the sermon. We would cause the army to come to life and then have the prophet prophesy to them.

But not here. No, God has Ezekiel speak his Word to them *while they are dead*, while they are dry bones. And as he speaks, they come to life. You see, this is illustrating the point that life comes by God's Word, as his Spirit ministers his Word to our hearts.

This is a particularly arresting picture because it's a bit like the way God called Ezekiel to speak to a people who wouldn't listen. This is the situation of the first three chapters of Ezekiel's prophecy. There, God called the prophet to a people who were like dry bones, who, God tells him, would not listen to him. But just as God himself had spoken into the void and by his power created all things, in this same way God re-creates, as it were, his people by his Word.

So God told Ezekiel here to speak to these dry bones. Life came by breath. Spirit traveled through speech. And that Word of God—his breath—gave life. So we see this close connection between life, breath, Spirit, speech, and Word.

We read of something similar in the ministry of our Lord in Mark 7. Some people had brought to Jesus a man who was deaf. And Jesus looked up to heaven and with a deep sigh said to the man, "Be opened" (Mark 7:34). At this, the man's ears were opened.

I love that verse. I love the image of Jesus speaking to a deaf man. Because I know that in my own life, when I was not a Christian, I was at enmity with God and God spoke to me. He spoke life where there was death. And Jesus, speaking to a deaf man here, did exactly the same thing. He brought life. Life came back to that man's ears.

So in the ministry of Jesus, we see Jesus calling his people to himself in just the way that Ezekiel prophesied. Ezekiel prophesied that God would give us a new heart and put a new spirit within us, taking away our heart of stone and giving us a heart of flesh (Ezek. 36:26). And that is exactly what Jesus does.

Well, if you are a Christian, you know that reality. You know what it means for God to put a fleshly heart in you, in the sense that the prophet describes. You know what it means to receive a heart that is spiritually alive. You know what it means to have a heart that is responsive to God and to his Word.

We Christians know that in and of ourselves we are spiritually dead apart from God's power. We know that we need God to make us alive. We need him to initiate his life-giving love to us through his Word and to reach down and to rip out our old stony heart and to give us a heart of flesh. We need a heart of love that is soft and supple and pliant to God's Word. And that is just what Jesus Christ does. He is creating a different kind of people—a people who show the life of God in them.

And this, of course, brings us to the supreme picture of the life-giving power of the Word of God in John 1:1–4. We read there,

In the beginning was the Word, and the Word was with God, and the Word was God. . . . All things were made through him, and without him was not any thing made that was made. In him was life, and the life was the light of men.

Supremely, then, the Word of God has come in Christ. It is in Christ that the Word of God has fully and finally come to us.

Jesus modeled this in his own ministry. Mark records for us that in the early days of Jesus' earthly ministry, his disciples came seeking him, telling him that many people had signed up for the conference, so to speak. Many people wanted to hear him teach. They were hanging on his words. Jesus, even in this short time recorded for us, had built a reputation for himself.

So the people were urging him, in effect, to come and perform miracles. After all, Jesus had done many signs, and people were responding by coming in huge numbers. But notice Jesus' response in Mark 1:38: "And he said to them, 'Let us go on to the next towns, that I may preach there also, for that is why I came out.'" So if you think preaching is just what some preachers are all about, listen to the Lord Jesus in Mark 1:38. A multitude has been clamoring to be ministered to physically, but Jesus says that he came to preach. He tells them that he came to bring God's Word.

God's Word Interprets His Actions

Now, if you keep reading in Mark's gospel, you see that Jesus knew that he had come fundamentally to lay down his life as a ransom for many (Mark 10:45). But in order for that sacrifice to be understood, he must first teach the people. And this is what God has always done, really. As you read through the Bible, you see that God acts and he interprets what he has done. God acts, but he does not just leave his act sitting out there to speak for itself. No, he then speaks to interpret his great saving acts.

This was a real weakness, I think, with some of the neoorthodox theology that was very prominent in our seminaries in the 1950s and 1960s, particularly when people would talk about "the great saving acts of God." G. Ernest Wright's book said things like that.[1] People were taught that God had moved in history. At this point, it is important to recall that neoorthodoxy purported to be a conservative movement, over and against the liberalism that just really dismissed all the supernatural claims about God.

Thus, the "God who acts" movement would seem to be a move in the right direction. But God's actions, without his interpretation to us of those actions, would be incomplete. Christ did not simply die on the cross as a mute Messiah; that was not God's plan at all. Rather, Christ was also a teacher who came to explain to us our sins and their connection with his death. And it is through this message that the Holy Spirit then brings life.

The speaking nature of God fits perfectly with the way that he has made us. Consider for a moment the importance of words in your own relationships. Our words are important for our relationships. This should cause no real argument.

The exchange of propositional truths (however that is done) between two people is part of what it means to be made in the image of God. This is one of the main places where Karl Barth was wrong. Barth talked about revelation as personal. He pitted the personal against the propositional, in other words. But propositional truths are at the very heart of any relationship.

1. G. Ernest Wright, *God Who Acts* (London: SCM, 1960).

Human communication is part of (and really at the very heart of) any and every relationship.

So should we be surprised that communication with God—from God to us—is at the heart of our relationship to him? Not at all. It makes complete sense. It is, after all, the way he has made us. Since we have separated ourselves from God by our sin, God must speak to us if we are to know him. God must reveal himself because we, on our own, as the result of our sin, would never know him otherwise. Either he speaks or we are forever lost in the darkness of our own speculations. But, praise God, he has spoken!

Consequently, we see in Romans 10 that faith comes from hearing the message, and the message is heard through the Word of Christ (Rom. 10:17). This Word of Christ is the message of the gospel. It is the message that God has made us in his image, but we have separated ourselves from him by our sin. God came in the flesh in the person of Christ, he lived a perfect life, and he died on the cross. He thus lived and died in place of all those who would ever repent of their sins and trust in him. And God raised him from the dead, gloriously, and he calls us now to repent of our sins and to trust in him.

That is the message about Christ. And since saving faith comes by hearing, we must give the primacy to the preaching of that Word by those whom God has specially called and gifted to carry out this glorious task. The Word of God brings life. God shows us that faith is central. And so the Word must be central because God's Holy Spirit creates his people by his Word.

The Inability of Human Schemes or Means

We can, of course, create our churches with other things at the core. We can do it around a fully graded choir program.

We can create a people around a successful building project or a denominational identity. We can create a people around a series of care groups, or a certain dress code that we all uphold. We can create a people around service to the community. We can create a people around opportunities for socializing for young mothers, or singles' or men's groups. We can even create a people around the personality of a preacher.

But we can see the people of God, his church, created only around the Word of God. Martin Luther, when asked how the Reformation had happened, said, "I simply taught, preached, wrote God's Word. Otherwise, I did nothing. The Word did it all." The Word of God brings life.

This brings us to the role of the preacher of God's Word. I recently read an article (not in a Christian magazine) that lamented the fact that many preachers today are driven by the audience and not the Word. They are driven by public opinion and not what God said.

If those of us who are called to preach speak about what is popular according to some poll, what good is that? What life does that bring? No, we are called to preach not merely moral exhortations, not merely history lessons about ancient Jerusalem, not mere social commentaries. Though any of these things may be part of the whole, we are primarily called to preach the Word of God to the church because God's Holy Spirit creates his people by his Word.

This is why when Paul wrote to Timothy, the young pastor whom he had discipled in Ephesus, he did not tell him to form a committee. He did not tell Timothy to take a survey or spend himself in visiting. Rather, the great final instruction from Paul to Timothy was straight and clear: "Preach the word" (2 Tim. 4:2).

It's a nice, brief imperative: "Preach the word." Paul's exhortation here is why the apostles had earlier determined, when there were problems with the equitable distribution of the financial aid in the church in Jerusalem, that they needed to find other people to solve those problems. Why? Because it was not right "that we should give up preaching the word of God to serve tables" (Acts 6:2).

I know that some today are suggesting that we need a less rational, more artistic, less authoritarian and elitist, more communal and participatory way of communicating God's truth than this ancient way of one person standing there giving a monologue, while others sit and listen in silence. Such a critique of preaching is being made by many today, including evangelical authors. I think the "ancient method" may be especially appropriate today, however, given our isolatingly subjectivist, anti-authority, confused and confusing culture. Given this, there is just something downright appropriate about God's people gathering and all closing their mouths, opening their ears, and listening to one person preach. Not just tell stories about his relationship with his kids and his dog, but actually preach God's Word to God's people.

I think this scenario is a perfect symbol of the way God brings life to us. We do not form it by consenting together to create life in a place. It is not in us to do that. It is God's work to bring life. We contribute nothing other than hearing and heeding the Word of God that is spoken to us.

Of course, there will come a day when faith will give way to sight and sermons will be no more. And I promise you as a preacher that nobody will think that day is more glorious than I! Revelation 22:4 is the climax of the Bible. And it is not about your ears. It is about your eyes. It presents that day when faith, wretched faith, will finally be thrown aside and will give way to sight.

We will, as the apostle says, see God. And he has made us with a longing for that day. There is a reason why our eyes have such ravenous appetites. They were made for the vision of God. They were made to see God!

For all the multimedia presentations and video clips that preachers use in their sermons, we must remember that we are not yet in that day when we can live by sight. We are in exile. We are in the "day of the ear," so to speak. We live by faith, and so like our first parents before us, like Noah and Abraham, like the Israelites and the ancient apostles in the New Testament, we rely on God's Word and we rely on God's Spirit.

Why Preaching Must Be Central

So what does this mean for our churches? Simply that the preaching of the Word must be absolutely central. Let me say it again: the preaching of God's Word must be absolutely central. After what we have studied, it shouldn't surprise you to hear that sound, expositional preaching of God's Word is often the fountainhead of the growth of the church, as it was in Martin Luther's own experience. Such careful attention to God's Word is the way to salvation—and often the beginning of reformation. God's Word is the word that we need to hear today.

We live in strange times, when even Christians who claim to be born again, who attend churches that claim to be evangelical, who say that the Bible is God's Word, ignore that very same Word. I remember when I was in England and a friend of mine went to a student ministry's chapter meeting. He came back to me just heartbroken. He recalled to me, "I was there and the singing went on for two hours. And the people, these young students, were crying out, 'O God, give us a word; speak to us, O Lord.'" And he said that the whole time their Bibles were lying there, closed, on their chairs.

This kind of thing deeply affects me. I'm not making a merely denominational point; I am quite happy for you to sing for two hours in your church if you have time for that. Moreover, I don't mind if people stand and raise their hands while they sing, if they feel so inclined.

What concerns me is when Christians are not taught to open the Word. They are not taught that, fundamentally, God has spoken to us in his Word and that Word is sufficient. It is all we need for life and for growth in grace and godliness. How do we instruct Christians to think about God's Word in these terms? By having the preaching of God's Word at the center of our churches.

Preaching should have certain content and should, at best, even have a certain transparency as to form. Preachers should preach God's Word, and church members should encourage them in preaching God's Word. If you're a church member reading this, wondering whether this applies to you, let me assure you that it does. This is because you have a terribly important role in affirming and encouraging your pastors to go in the direction for which I have been arguing. If you see your preacher going off after fads, kindly stop him. Pray. I say this gently, but cause him to feel bad about it when he goes to bed at night. Pray that God will give him a longing to know him better. He will soon find that he can only do so fundamentally through his Word, as the Spirit uses that Word in the minister's own heart. Pray that your minister will have a burning desire to bring God's Word to you, one of God's people. The truth of the preached Word, then, is what we desperately need.

So what is it that makes for a really good church? More than parking and pews and greeting and programs and nurseries and music and even more than the preacher, it is what is preached—the Word of God.

7

The Accessible Word

PHILIP GRAHAM RYKEN

So shall my word be that goes out from my mouth;
it shall not return to me empty. (Isaiah 55:11)

THE PROTESTANT REFORMERS are well known for their famous doctrine of *sola Scriptura*: the Bible alone is our only ultimate authority for faith and practice—not the pope, or the church, or the traditions of men, or the subjective insights of the individual believer, but the Bible alone.

It is also well known that this doctrinal principle of *sola Scriptura* was closely joined to a practical strategy for spreading the Reformation across Europe. That strategy was to give people the Bible in their own language. Throughout the Middle Ages the church had been worshiping primarily in Latin, which was the language of scholars, but not the language of the man on the street or the person in the pew. Yet the Reformers were absolutely convinced that in order for the Holy Spirit to do his life-changing work, people needed to hear the Word of God in words they could understand.

Communicating the Word of God in words that people could understand was the burning passion of William Tyndale, the Bible translator whose lifework was to put the Scriptures of the Old and New Testaments into English. Tyndale once found himself in the company of a learned scholar. Before long their conversation turned into a spirited debate, and eventually Tyndale drove the man to the point where he said that the people would be better off not having the law of God at all, but only listening to the pope. Tyndale responded by saying, "I defy the Pope and all his laws, and if God spare my life ere many years, I will cause a boy that driveth the plough, shall know more of the scripture than thou dost."[1]

By the grace of God, Tyndale achieved his ambition. By the time he died, Tyndale had translated most of the Bible into English, and people all over the country—not just the rich, but also the poor—were able to read and understand the Bible for themselves.

Tragically, Tyndale was condemned for heresy by Henry VIII, strangled, and then burned at the stake. But as far as Tyndale himself was concerned, death was only a small price to pay for making the Bible accessible to people in English. This is what he wrote to the king's chief minister, at a time when he was living in Europe and hiding from the king's wrath:

> I assure you, if it would stand with the king's most gracious
> pleasure to grant only a bare text of the scripture to be out

1. William Tyndale, quoted in David Daniell, *William Tyndale: A Biography* (New Haven, CT: Yale University Press, 1994), 79.

forth among his people . . . , be it of the translation of what person soever shall please his majesty, I shall immediately make faithful promise never to write more, not abide two days in these parts after the same: but immediately to repair unto his realm, and there most humbly submit myself at the feet of his royal majesty, offering my body to suffer what pain or torture, yea, what death his grace will, so this be obtained. And till that time, I will abide the asperity of all chances, whatsocvcr shall come, and endure my life in as many pains as it is able to bear and suffer.[2]

William Tyndale was committed to giving people the Bible at all costs. Nothing was more important—not even the price of a man's life. In making this calculation, he was making a crucial assumption. That assumption, which is a major principle in the evangelical doctrine of Scripture, happens to be under attack in our day. Tyndale was assuming that when the Bible is read, it can be understood. He was assuming the accessibility, or the clarity, or what a theologian would call the *perspicuity* of Scripture.

Attacks on Perspicuity

The doctrine of perspicuity is under attack.[3] Casting aspersions on the clarity of Scripture is almost as old as the world itself. Consider the diabolical question that Satan asked Eve in the garden of Eden: "Did God *actually* say, 'You shall not eat of any tree in the garden'?" (Gen. 3:1). This was partly an attack on God's authority, of course, but it was also an attack on the perspicuity of his Word. The serpent was looking for some

2. Ibid., 216.
3. This section of the chapter was improved by wise comments from Jeff Greenman, who is Associate Dean of Biblical and Theological Studies at Wheaton College.

wiggle room, tempting Eve to think that there might be some ambiguity in the clear Word of God.

Who is attacking the perspicuity of the Bible today? This doctrine is still under attack from the Roman Catholic Church. If the meaning of Scripture were clear in itself, there would be no need for an infallible teaching magisterium to make its meaning clear. As it is, however, the Catholic Church does not believe that the Bible, apart from any outside information or authority, is sufficient to explain all essential points of doctrine.[4] Scripture alone is insufficient; to understand what Scripture says, we also need the traditions and the teachings of the church. To be sure, there is much that we can learn from the community of faith, down through the ages, about how to interpret and apply Scripture. But Catholicism goes beyond this to say that the authoritative interpretation of the Roman Catholic Church is as necessary as the Word of God itself. In addition to an infallible Bible, we need an infallible interpretation of the Bible.

A different sort of attack comes from some leaders in the emerging church. Brian McLaren, for example, criticizes an older view of the Bible as providing a definite plan for getting to heaven and a clear, unambiguous rule for right and wrong behavior. The Bible does not provide that kind of clarity, nor does it claim to do so.[5] What is important about the Bible is not its authority, inerrancy, infallibility, or objectivity—after all, McLaren says, these doctrinal terms are not even found in Scripture—but primarily its utility.[6] Others like to emphasize the ambiguity of Scripture. In all humility, they say, we should be less dogmatic about what the Bible teaches. Yet rather than

4. See Norman L. Geisler and Ralph E. MacKenzie, *Roman Catholics and Evangelicals: Agreements and Differences* (Grand Rapids: Baker, 1995), 178, 182, 190.
5. Brian D. McLaren, *A Generous Orthodoxy* (Grand Rapids: Zondervan, 2004), 160.
6. Ibid., 164.

inspiring more confidence in the clear truth of Scripture, the result of this approach is to introduce doubt where there ought to be certainty and hesitation where there ought to be confidence in what the Bible says.

Then there are all the attacks—whether implicit or explicit—that come from people who make their living by studying and teaching the Bible. Some Bible scholars (not all, of course) give the impression that the Bible is not clear in itself, but becomes clear only when we know the historical, archaeological, or cultural background to the biblical text. Of course there is a place for careful biblical scholarship, which often gives us a deeper understanding of the Scriptures by helping us to see what is really there in the biblical text. But some scholars go beyond this by claiming that scholarly expertise is essential to understanding the Scriptures.

These attacks on the perspicuity of the Bible find a ready audience in these postmodern times, when many people doubt whether anything is absolutely true at all. If we claim to have a clear word from God, then obviously we are intolerant and possibly dangerous. There is no such thing as the plain meaning of any text; there are always multiple interpretations. Everything is open to question, including the very possibility of clear communication.

One is reminded of a scene in the first act of Robert Bolt's famous play *A Man for All Seasons*. Sir Thomas More is arguing with Henry VIII about whether the king has the right to divorce his wife. Henry is arguing that since his wife had been married to his brother, his marriage is biblically illegitimate and ought to be annulled, making him free to marry yet another wife. More responds by arguing that two wrongs do not make a right. Yet both men are arguing on the basis of a text from Scripture. Here is how their argument comes to its climax:

The king says, "You must consider, Thomas, that I stand in peril of my soul. It was no marriage; she was my brother's widow. Leviticus: 'Thou shalt not uncover the nakedness of thy brother's wife.' Leviticus, Chapter eighteen, Verse sixteen."

"Yes, Your Grace," says Thomas More. "But Deuteronomy—"

To which Henry triumphantly replies, "Deuteronomy's ambiguous!"[7]

Arguments against Perspicuity

Is the Bible ambiguous or not? Does it have a plain meaning—a meaning that people can understand? Yes, it does. But before defining and defending the doctrine of the perspicuity of Scripture, we should consider some of the strongest objections to it.

In his excellent book *A Clear and Present Word*, the Australian theologian Mark Thompson mentions five specific arguments that people have given for saying that Scripture is not accessible to our understanding.[8]

First, there is an argument based on *the nature of God*—an argument that Erasmus made against Martin Luther. God himself is a transcendent mystery; he is greater than the human mind. "Who has known the mind of the Lord . . . ?" Scripture asks (Rom. 11:34, quoting Isa. 40:13). "How inscrutable his ways!" (Rom. 11:33). To say that Scripture is clear, therefore, when it speaks of such a transcendent God is presumptuous. Erasmus contrasted the "unsearchable majesty of the divine wisdom" with "the weakness of the human mind" and concluded that many things about God will always remain obscure.[9]

---

7. Robert Bolt, *A Man for All Seasons* (1960; repr., New York: Vintage, 1990), 54.

8. Mark D. Thompson, *A Clear and Present Word: The Clarity of Scripture*, New Studies in Biblical Theology (Downers Grove, IL: InterVarsity Press, 2006).

9. Erasmus, *De libero arbitrio diatribe sive collatio*, quoted in ibid., 144.

Second, there is an argument based on *the role of the church*. As we have seen, traditionally this is a Roman Catholic argument against the perspicuity of Scripture. To interpret the Scriptures properly, we need an authoritative interpretation from the one true church. In the words of the Council of Trent, the "Holy Mother Church" has the responsibility to "pass judgment on the true meaning and interpretation of the Sacred Scriptures."[10] This is still the official position of the Roman Catholic Church today, for according to Vatican II, "The task of authentically interpreting the word of God, whether written or handed on, has been entrusted *exclusively* to the living teaching office of the Church."[11]

Third, there is an argument based on *the humanity of Scripture*. Although Scripture is a divine word, it is also written in human words. In acknowledging the genuine humanity of the biblical text, we need to recognize that human language is an intrinsically fallible means of communication. There is always ambiguity and lack of clarity in human speech. Therefore, it is unrealistic to expect the Bible to speak clearly. In Scripture, fallible men have spoken the Word of God in fallible human words. The Old and New Testaments do not have a special quality that is lacking in other forms of human writing. If we are to be honest about the messy historical realities of the biblical text, we need to admit that Scripture is not perspicuous.

Fourth, there is an argument based on *the variety of interpretations*. It is simply a fact that not everyone reads the Bible the same way. How can we say, then, that Scripture is clear? This standard Roman Catholic argument against the doctrine of the clarity of Scripture has gained added currency in postmodern times. There are many conflicting interpretations of Scripture,

10. Council of Trent, Session 4 (April 8, 1546).
11. Vatican II, *Dei verbum*, 2.10 (emphasis added).

just as there are many perspectives on reality. If Scripture is clear, then why do so many learned men and women disagree about what it means?

Finally, there is an argument based on *the teaching of Scripture*. Here the argument is that the Bible itself indicates that it is obscure. Consider the teaching that Jesus gave his disciples on the road to Emmaus, when "he interpreted to them in all the Scriptures the things concerning himself" (Luke 24:27). If these things were clear, then why did the disciples need so much help to understand them? We may ask the same question about the Ethiopian eunuch whom Philip met on the road to Africa—the man who asked for an explanation of Isaiah 53 (see Acts 8:30–35). If what Isaiah said about the Suffering Servant was a clear prophecy about Jesus Christ, then why did the Ethiopian need someone like Philip to explain it?

Defining the Doctrine

These arguments are too weighty to dismiss out of hand, especially because some of them are based on Scripture itself. Nevertheless, we may have confidence and joy in the clarity of Scripture. The Bible is a book that we can understand. It is not so hopelessly confusing or ambiguous that we need someone or something else to make its meaning clear. It is a book that we can read for ourselves and that even the simplest person can comprehend.

So what do we mean by the perspicuity or accessibility of Scripture? We mean that the Bible's basic message is clear. We mean that the central gospel of salvation in Christ is accessible to anyone who reads or hears the Word of God. Or, to say this in the way the apostle Paul said it, the Scriptures "*are able* to make you wise for salvation through faith in Christ Jesus" (2 Tim. 3:15).

We also mean that human beings can know and understand what the Bible mainly says about the way to live—the Scriptures are clear about the essentials of the Christian life as well as the essentials of the Christian faith. Therefore, the Old and New Testaments can and should be read by ordinary people everywhere. As Martin Luther said, "everything there is in the Scriptures has been brought out by the Word into the most definite light, and published to all the world."[12] Luther also said, "The meaning of Scripture is, in and of itself, so certain, accessible and clear that Scripture interprets itself and tests, judges and illuminates everything else."[13]

This does not eliminate the need for people to study and teach the Bible, as if people always immediately understood everything the Bible says. This is obvious from some of the scriptural examples that we have already mentioned. When Jesus walked to Emmaus with his disciples on that first Easter afternoon, for example, he explained what was said in all the Scriptures concerning himself. The disciples needed further instruction. But notice that Jesus gave them this instruction from Scripture itself, and not from something beyond Scripture. Similarly, Philip helped the Ethiopian eunuch by giving him the hermeneutical key to Isaiah 53. The man's problem was not that he did not understand the words, but that he did not know the Savior to whom they referred.

There is always a place for this kind of teaching both inside and outside the church, in discipleship as well as evangelism. The doctrine of the perspicuity of Scripture has never denied the legitimate place of Bible teaching. In order to have a fuller

12. Martin Luther, quoted in Thompson, *A Clear and Present Word*, 149.
13. Ibid., 144.

understanding of Scripture, the people of God need the explanation and application of what it says. In his masterful *Disputations on Holy Scripture*, written late in the sixteenth century, the Cambridge scholar William Whitaker said:

> Our fundamental principles are these: First, that the Scriptures are sufficiently clear to admit of their being read by the people and the unlearned with some fruit and utility. Secondly, that all things necessary to salvation are propounded in plain words in the Scriptures. Meanwhile, we concede that there are many obscure places, and that the Scriptures need explication; and that, on this account, God's ministers are to be listened to when they expound the word of God, and the men best skilled in Scripture are to be consulted.[14]

The successful exposition of Scripture depends, in part, on its perspicuity. How could anyone explain the Scriptures, or understand the Scriptures that are being explained, unless the Scriptures themselves were clear enough for both the preacher and the congregation to understand them? Preachers and teachers and Bible commentators are not necessary to understand the text at all, but they can deepen our understanding—not by telling us something different from what the Bible says, but by helping us to see what is really there.

Nor does the doctrine of the clarity of Scripture deny that some parts of the Bible are harder to understand than others. Believing that the Bible is clear in its central saving message and its application to life does not mean that all its parts are equally accessible, as though we would never have any difficulty understanding some passages in the Bible. Even the apostle Peter

14. William Whitaker, *Disputations on Holy Scripture* (1588; repr., Morgan, PA: Soli Deo Gloria, 2000), 364.

found some parts of the Bible hard to understand. He says as much at the end of his second epistle, when he is commenting on the letters of Paul, his fellow apostle. "There are some things in them that are hard to understand," Peter admitted, "which the ignorant and unstable twist to their own destruction, as they do the other Scriptures" (2 Peter 3:16).

This text is sometimes used to attack the perspicuity of Scripture. But in fact it is clear that Peter believed in this doctrine as much as anyone else. As much as he loved Paul's letters, Peter was not about to pretend that understanding them is always easy. Yet at the same time he tells his readers to study Paul's letters and thus avoid the errors of lawless men. The letters of Paul "are not so difficult that they should be put aside." After all, Peter has just "made an appeal to them in support of what he has been saying, which presumably indicates that he understood what Paul was saying at some point." Indeed, his entire argument "assumes that the proper meaning of Paul's words can be identified and contrasted with what these people are suggesting. Furthermore, Peter seems to assume that the recipients of his letter are in a position to make this identification and draw this contrast. How else could they avoid the error?"[15]

In understanding the hard places in Scripture, we are wise to apply the important principle of letting Scripture interpret Scripture. As Martin Luther said, "Scripture is its own interpreter."[16] If we follow this principle, then our interpretation of Scripture is controlled by Scripture itself, not by something outside of Scripture. Whenever we read something that is hard to understand, we should look at what the Bible says somewhere else to gain greater clarity. Generally speaking, something that is difficult for us to understand in one passage is stated more simply somewhere

15. Thompson, *A Clear and Present Word*, 108.
16. Martin Luther, quoted in ibid., 137.

else in Scripture. Here is how Augustine explained this principle: "The Holy Spirit has generously and advantageously planned Holy Scripture in such a way that in the easier passages He relieves our hunger; in the more obscure He drives away our pride. Practically nothing is dug out from those obscure texts which is not discovered to be said very plainly in another place."[17]

There is something else that the perspicuity of Scripture does not deny, which is that some readers understand the Bible better than others. The Bible is not equally clear in all places, and it is not equally clear to all people. As William Whitaker once said, "There is nothing in Scripture so plain that some men have not doubted it."[18]

Varying interpretations of Scripture arise in part because we all have different gifts and abilities. It is also because, for all its simplicity, the Bible has profound depths of meaning. Gregory the Great said that just as the Bible

> exercises the wise by means of mysteries, so it usually revives the simple by means of what lies on the surface. It holds in the open that by which little ones may be nourished and keeps hidden that by which those of lofty intellect might stand in wonder. It is, so to speak, a kind of river, if I may so liken it, which is both shallow and deep, in which both the lamb may find a footing and the elephant swim.[19]

There is another, darker reason why some people do not understand the Bible as well as others. It is not only because some people are lambs, but also because some people are goats. They are not among the sheep that Jesus says will always listen

17. Augustine, *De doctrina Christiana*, 2.6(8), quoted in ibid., 110.
18. Whitaker, *Disputations on Holy Scripture*, 389.
19. Gregory the Great, *Moralia in Iob*, quoted in Thompson, *A Clear and Present Word*, 110.

to his voice (John 10:27). They do not believe in the God of the Bible or have a saving relationship with Jesus Christ. As a result, they do not have a clear understanding of the Bible, as clear as it is. They misconstrue the meaning of Scripture, misunderstand the gospel of salvation, and misapply the law of God. Then they attack the Bible for its alleged mistakes. But the problem is with them and not with the Scriptures themselves, the truth of which can be understood only by faith.

William Whitaker used a simple analogy to explain why the inability of some people to understand the Bible does not deny the Bible's clarity. "A lamp hath light in itself, whether men look upon that light or not: so also the Scripture is clear and perspicuous," Whitaker said, "whether men be illuminated by it, or receive from it no light whatever."[20]

Unless and until we believe, there is a darkness in us that prevents us from seeing the light. As it says in the Gospel of John, "the light has come into the world, and people loved the darkness rather than the light" (John 3:19). This spiritual darkness is what keeps people from understanding the plain meaning of Scripture, which can be received only by faith. In short, Scripture itself is clear; it is our own darkness that needs to be illuminated. "If our gospel is veiled," said the apostle Paul, "it is veiled only to those who are perishing" (2 Cor. 4:3). Only those who are alive in Christ can see and understand what Scripture says.

The believer's ability to see the light of Scripture is a gift of the third person of the Trinity. God has not given us his Word without also giving us his Spirit—the Spirit who guides us into all truth (John 16:13). Martin Luther said that there is an internal clarity—the clarity of the Word as we perceive it—that can come only from the illumination of the Spirit:

20. Whitaker, *Disputations on Holy Scripture*, 384.

"no man perceives one iota of what is in the Scriptures unless he has the Spirit of God."[21]

The Character of God

Thus far we have been defining the perspicuity of Scripture against various attacks that have been made and are being made against this great doctrine. We have been trying to understand what theologians do and do not mean when they talk about the clarity and accessibility of the Bible.

We turn now to defending the doctrine we have been defining by giving two of the main reasons we can be sure that the Bible is clear in its essential message. One argument is from the character of God, while the other is from the testimony of Scripture.

The character of God is always the right place to begin. He is the basis for all reality and the foundation of all truth. When we base any argument on his character, therefore, at least we know that we are beginning in the right place, which gives us an opportunity to end up at the right place, too. God is an especially good place to begin when we are talking about the doctrine of Scripture. God himself is the Author of every word in Scripture. It only makes sense to say, therefore, that what we read in the Bible bears witness to his character, telling us something about *who he is*.

One of the most obvious things the Bible shows about God is that he communicates. Our God is a speaking God. We see this both at the very beginning and at the very end of the Bible. God speaks, and the universe comes into being. The first chapter

21. Martin Luther, quoted in Thompson, *A Clear and Present Word*, 149.

of the Bible begins with a record of what God said, and then what he created as a result. God also speaks in the last chapter of Scripture, telling us what will happen soon, at the final coming of the Lord Jesus Christ (see Rev. 22:20).

What is true of the beginning and the end of the Bible is also true of the middle. Scripture is full of God speaking—not simply in the sense that God speaks all the words of Scripture, but also in the sense that Scripture records many occasions when God said something to his people. God spoke to Adam and Eve in the garden, warning them about the forbidden fruit, and then later pronouncing judgment on their sins and announcing the first promise of salvation. God spoke to Noah, commanding him to build an ark. God spoke to Abraham, calling him to a life of pilgrim faith and promising him a land and a people to be his everlasting inheritance. God spoke to Moses in fire and smoke, giving the law. We hear God's voice again and again throughout the Old Testament. He is constantly warning, exhorting, rebuking, promising, and comforting. Our God is a speaking God; he is always saying something.

God spoke again with the coming of Christ. People sometimes wonder why there is such a long historical gap between the Old Testament and the New Testament. Perhaps it is because God wanted to make sure that his people heard his voice. They waited long centuries for another prophet. For faithful believers, this served to heighten a sense of expectation. When would God speak again?

After centuries of silence, God spoke in the ministry of his Son. When Jesus came up out of the water at his baptism, a voice from heaven said, "This is my beloved Son, with whom I am well pleased" (Matt. 3:17). The same voice spoke on the Mount of Transfiguration: "This is my beloved Son . . . ; listen to him" (Matt. 17:5). God spoke again before the passion of the Christ: "I have glorified [my name]," the voice said, "and I will glorify it again" (John 12:28).

God was also speaking through Christ. Although the earthly ministry of Jesus was partly a ministry of healing, fundamentally it was a ministry of speaking. Jesus began his public ministry by proclaiming the gospel of God, opening the Scriptures and preaching a kingdom message of faith and repentance (see Mark 1:14–15; Luke 4:16–21). When people wanted Jesus to be a full-time wonder-worker, he said that he had not come to heal, but to preach (Mark 1:38). This teaching ministry had a powerful sanctifying influence on his disciples—so much so that Jesus was able to say to them, "You are clean because of the word that I have spoken to you" (John 15:3). Jesus kept preaching this cleansing Word until he went to the cross, and then continued to preach it from the cross itself. Until his dying breath, he was speaking the Word of God.

Whether we read the Old Testament or the New Testament—whenever we read the Bible—we hear the voice of a speaking God. In fact, the writer to the Hebrews described the entire history of salvation in terms of what God has said. "God spoke to our fathers by the prophets," the Scriptures say, summarizing the Old Testament, "but in these last days he has spoken to us by his Son" (Heb. 1:1–2).

The reason God speaks to us is that he wants us to know him for eternal life. God not only does things for our salvation, but also says things, and the things he says help us to understand the things that he has done. The whole Bible is telling us that God wants us to know who he is.

Now, can God be understood, or not? Can he get his message across to us clearly? Is the Bible perspicuous enough for us to know God and to understand what he is saying? Yes, we can take God at his Word. God speaks to us because he wants to communicate with us, and his Word is effective for that purpose. Consider the bold promise of Isaiah 55:

> For as the rain and the snow come down from heaven
>   and do not return there but water the earth,
> making it bring forth and sprout,
>   giving seed to the sower and bread to the eater,
> so shall my word be that goes out from my mouth;
>   it shall not return to me empty,
> but it shall accomplish that which I purpose,
>   and shall succeed in the thing for which I sent it.
>   (Isa. 55:10–11)

According to Isaiah, the Word of God really does something in the world. The only Word that can fulfill that promise is a clear and accessible Word. Furthermore, any attack on the perspicuity of Scripture is really an attack on God himself. If Scripture is not clear, then God is not clear. If his Word cannot be understood, then either God does not want us to know him (which would make him a liar) or else he is not an effective communicator. It is not just our doctrine of Scripture that is at stake in this discussion, therefore, but also our doctrine of God.

Martin Luther pointed out that if the meaning of Scripture is not clear, then God has given us Scripture in vain. "If Scripture is obscure or ambiguous," Luther said, "what point is there in God giving it to us? Are we not obscure and ambiguous enough without having our own obscurity, ambiguity, and darkness augmented for us from heaven?"[22] William Whitaker used similar logic when he argued that any attack on the clarity of Scripture is tantamount to an attack on the Holy Spirit:

22. Ibid., 147.

If the Scriptures are so obscure and difficult to be understood, that they cannot be read with advantage by the people, then this hath happened, either because the Holy Spirit could not write more plainly, or because he would not. No one will say that he could not: and that he would not, is repugnant to the end of writing. . . . The Holy Spirit willed the Scriptures to be consigned to writing in order that we might understand them; and that this was the end which he proposed there are many things in the Scriptures themselves that testify: therefore, they are so written as to be intelligible by us, or else the Holy Spirit hath not gained his end; which cannot be thought without impiety.[23]

Instead of impugning the character of God by attacking the clarity of his Word, we should believe in the goodness of God and then reason from there to the perspicuity of Scripture. As Mark Thompson has written, "The ultimate guarantee that God's word will be heard and understood, that it will achieve the purpose for which it was spoken and written, is the power and goodness of God himself."[24]

In these postmodern times we are often told that language is problematic, that in any conversation there is a loss of meaning. Sometimes we are even told that true communication is impossible. But the Bible views language as a gift from God, who in his grace has accommodated himself to our understanding by speaking in a way that we can understand. God speaks so that we can know him—specifically, so that we can know him unto salvation. To that end, he has given us a gospel: a spoken message that serves as an announcement of good news. This message is something

23. Whitaker, *Disputations on Holy Scripture*, 392.
24. Thompson, *A Clear and Present Word*, 111.

that we can understand. The gospel of Jesus Christ is "the gospel of God" (Rom. 1:1), the good news that God has spoken for our salvation.

Here, then, is another thing at stake in the perspicuity of Scripture: not only the doctrine of Scripture, but also our own personal salvation. Is the saving Word of God something that we can understand, or not? If not, then how will we be saved?

The slave trader John Newton wrestled with this issue when his soul was in turmoil and he wondered whether any of God's amazing grace could save a wretch like him. Newton was caught in a violent storm at sea. He went belowdecks to man the pumps. It was such a desperate situation that Newton began to pray for the mercy of God. In the following days, as the storm continued, he searched the Scriptures for some encouraging word from God. Newton was not altogether clear about the way of salvation, and he had no assurance of eternal life. Then he came to Luke 11:13, where he read that the heavenly Father would give the Holy Spirit to those who ask him. Newton said, "If this book be true, the promise in this passage must be true likewise. I have need of that very Spirit, by which the whole was written, in order to understand it aright. He has engaged here to give that Spirit to those who ask: I must therefore pray for it; and, if it be of God, he will make good on his own word."[25]

As John Newton discovered, God always makes good on his Word. He does this because he is a good God, who loves to make his message clear enough for us to believe in Jesus Christ and receive the free gift of eternal life.

25. John Newton, *Memoirs of Rev. John Newton*, as quoted by Derek W. H. Thomas in a newsletter from the First Presbyterian Church in Jackson, Mississippi (2006).

The Testimony of Scripture

Thus far we have considered one argument for the clarity of Scripture—an argument based on the character of God. But what does the Bible say about itself? Rather than imposing our doctrine *on* the Bible, we want to get our doctrine *from* the Bible. So can we demonstrate the doctrine of biblical perspicuity from the testimony of Scripture?

One way to answer this question is to look at the way in which Jesus and his apostles treated the Word of God. When they referred to a Scripture passage from the Old Testament, as they so often did, did they treat it as something unclear and ambiguous, or as something that people could readily understand? The answer is obvious, of course. Their appeal to the Old Testament was always definitive. Some twenty-five hundred verses in the New Testament either quote from or allude to the Old Testament. In every case, the appeal to Scripture is decisive. It always settles the argument—Scripture is just that clear. Why else would Jesus and his apostles refer to the Old Testament, if not to give a clear word from God? The assumption in every case is that the meaning of the Bible is perspicuous. The certainty of these men in quoting from the Old Testament assumed the clarity of those Scriptures.

To give just one example, consider the way that Jesus answered Satan when he was tempted in the wilderness (Matt. 4:1–11). We cannot help but be impressed with the way that Jesus resisted every temptation: he did it simply by wielding the strong sword of the Word of God. For each diabolical temptation he had an appropriate response straight from the book of Deuteronomy. We do not find Jesus holding back because he was not entirely sure what the Old Testament meant. Nor do we hear him saying, "You know, Satan, there are several different ways to interpret this passage." On the contrary, each time we hear Jesus give a decisive quotation that assumes the clarity of Scripture.

Many other biblical texts bear witness to the Bible's confidence in its own clarity. Consider what Moses said about the law that God had given on the mountain. The prophet was coming to the end of his life, and with his famous last words he wanted to remind the people of God what role the Scriptures would have in their daily lives. Moses had given them the law of God. He had told them to read it publicly, to teach it to their children, and to live by it all their days. But this assumed that the law was something they could understand and obey. So Moses said:

> This commandment that I command you today is not . . . far off. It is not in heaven, that you should say, "Who will ascend to heaven for us and bring it to us, that we may hear it and do it?" Neither is it beyond the sea, that you should say, "Who will go over the sea for us and bring it to us, that we may hear it and do it?" But the word is very near you. It is in your mouth and in your heart, so that you can do it. (Deut. 30:11–14)

What Moses said about the law is something that we can also say about the gospel. It is not somewhere out of reach; it is not up in heaven or across the sea. Rather, it is somewhere close to the heart, so that we can believe it and live by it.

Or consider what the poet said in Psalm 119—the long psalm on the law of God: "Your word is a lamp to my feet and a light to my path" (Ps. 119:105). This classic proof for the perspicuity of Scripture is precious to me because I learned it in kindergarten and have taught it to my own children. What a marvelous gift to give a young child! It is a verse to build a life upon, because it tells us that the Word of God will light our pathway through life. The verse is also an example of the very thing that it is talking about. The verse is so clear that even a little child can understand it. As the psalmist said a little later in the same psalm: "The unfolding of your words gives light; it imparts understanding to the simple" (119:130). What enables us to see things clearly is the clear Word of God.

Many other texts confirm that the Bible believes in its own accessibility. Mark Thompson cites 2 Kings 22 as making a strong case for the perspicuity of Scripture. There we read about the rediscovery of the Book of the Law under King Josiah. This part of the Word of God had been lost for many years, before it was rediscovered in the temple by Hilkiah the high priest. When Hilkiah's secretary Shaphan read the words of that Scripture to Josiah, the king tore his clothes and said, "Great is the wrath of the LORD that is kindled against us, because our fathers have not obeyed the words of this book, to do according to all that is written concerning us" (2 Kings 22:13). The king knew that his people were under the judgment of God, and this brought him to immediate repentance. He did not need to get a bunch of scholars together and hold a consultation to tell him what the Bible meant. He understood what Scripture said—it was just that clear.

Something similar happened when Nehemiah rebuilt the city of Jerusalem after the exile and Ezra read the people God's law in the square in front of the Water Gate. Ezra and his scribes opened the Scriptures and read them from morning until noon. The Scriptures were read to "the men and the women and those who could understand" (Neh. 8:3). In other words, the Word of God was read to the men, women, and children—children who were old enough to understand the reading of God's Word. This public reading of Scripture, which was followed by the exposition of Ezra and the other priests, proceeded on the assumption that people could understand what it said—that its meaning was clear. And in fact, the people did understand. As Scripture says, "the ears of all the people were attentive to the Book of the Law" (8:3).

Using God's Clear Word

Ezra gives us a good example to follow. We have a clear text from a good God. It is a text we can use for our own daily Bible reading. As we read the Scriptures, we can understand what they say and the Holy Spirit will use them to make us more like Christ.

What are some of the ways that we can make good use of God's Word? We can use it with our children. As soon as they can understand any words at all, they can begin to understand the true words of God, and God will use those words to grow them in the knowledge of his Son.

Because the Bible is clear, we can use it in ministry, starting with evangelism. We do not need to use our own supposedly simpler words to explain the Christian faith, but we can use the very words of God, which have the power to bring people to saving faith. We can use the Word of God in our teaching and preaching. We do not need to spend all our time telling stories or sharing our own spiritual experiences. The Bible is clear enough for the people of God to understand. It is also clear enough to use for systematic theology. In fact, without the doctrine of the perspicuity of Scripture, we would not have any doctrine at all. This doctrine is essential to all the other doctrines, because unless the Bible is clear, we cannot do any further theology.

The Bible is equally clear about the ethical challenges of our society. It is clear on the sanctity of life—that abortion is the taking of a human life. It is clear on gender relationships—that in the wisdom of God men and women have full equality and divinely ordained complementarity. It is clear on adultery and homosexuality—that the only pure expression of sexual intimacy is shared between one man and one woman who are joined in a love covenant for life. The Bible is clear about caring for the poor, pursuing war with justice, exercising the godly stewardship of our possessions, and everything else in life.

It is because the Bible is so clear that it is so useful. God will make it clear to us as we trust in him for clarity. The prayer of Psalm 119:18 is a prayer that God loves to answer, by the power of his Holy Spirit: "Open my eyes, that I may behold wondrous things out of your law." In light of the coming of Christ, we might paraphrase this verse to say: "Open my eyes, that I may behold wondrous things out of your gospel."

What a difference the Word of God makes when our eyes are opened and we clearly see what it so clearly says. One missionary visited a man and his wife in a remote country in central Asia.[26] The man had been studying English, and at a certain point he quietly asked one of his friends in the class for a Bible. He did not go to church or attend a Bible study. He simply read the Bible for himself, and as he read, he said in his heart, "This is life! This is truth!"

The man's wife noticed that he had been reading a Bible, but their culture is so hostile to Christianity that this was not something they could discuss openly. It had to be kept a secret. The woman was curious, however, so she secretly went out and purchased her own Bible on the underground market. When she brought it home and began to read it, she said in her heart, "This is life! This is truth!"

26. This story comes from a firsthand account in a CrossWorld newsletter written by Lisa Weidman (February 2006).

For months the man and his wife did not discuss what they were learning from the Bible. But eventually they shared their faith in Jesus with each other. The difference in their lives was dramatic. Instead of arguing all the time, they started singing together—something no one else in their community ever did. Without any formal Bible training, they began to put what they were reading into practice. The Word of God taught them to see the needs of the poor. They gathered some of the older women in their community together and taught them how to clean and repair old sandals. As they worked with these women, they began to share the gospel, and most of them came to faith in Christ. Then they saw young teenagers falling behind in life, so they started an educational center, where today they provide not only teaching, but also prayer and spiritual instruction.

Because of their faith in Christ, the man and his wife often receive threats from their neighbors and from the local authorities. But they are continuing to serve the Lord. They are doing this because the Word is clear to them about God, about salvation, and about loving their neighbors in the name of Jesus Christ. As the missionary left the couple's home, she could hear their voices follow her out into the street, singing praises to their God.

We should consider what the clear Word of God is doing in our own lives. Is it giving us joy in the truth? Is it giving us love for our family? Is it promoting a heart for the poor? Is it putting a song into our lives? The Bible ought to be doing all these things for us, and in us, and through us. As Peter testified, we have a clear and certain Word from God "to which [we] will do well to pay attention as to a lamp shining in a dark place, until the day dawns and the morning star rises in [our] hearts" (2 Peter 1:19).

8

Preaching: The Means of Revival

EDMUND P. CLOWNEY

Is not my word like fire, declares the LORD, and like
a hammer that breaks the rock in pieces?
(Jer. 23:29)

ONE OF THE THINGS that the Word of God (specifically, the Word of God preached) accomplishes by God's sovereign blessing is revival. The question that may be raised, then, is this: Has preaching had it? And this raises another question, too: Has revival had it? Maybe these are the same questions. The decline of preaching and the state of the church of Jesus Christ are factors that are surely related to each other.

131

Learning from George Whitefield

Preaching has been the principal means for revival; that is perfectly clear in the history of revivals. One of the great figures in the history of revivals in America is George Whitefield. We can therefore learn much about preaching and its relationship to revival by studying his journals. I would like to examine just a few of Whitefield's journal entries. The first was from the year 1739, shortly before Whitefield came to the United States, when he was roughly twenty-four years old. On March 14, when he was at Bath in England, he records that he was forbidden to preach at a local prison. He writes, "Being resolved not to give place to my adversaries . . . I preached at Baptist Mills, a place very near the city." He preached to three or four thousand people from these words: "What think you of Christ?" (see Matt. 22:42).[1] And then he wrote, "Blessed be God, all things happen for the furtherance of the gospel. I now preach to ten times more people than I should, if I had been confined to the churches. Surely the devil is blind, and so are his emissaries, or otherwise they would not thus confound themselves."[2] Whitefield was banned from churches but found himself preaching to larger crowds precisely because of this fact!

Next, we read an entry from Sunday, March 18, a few days after the previous entry. Here, he writes concerning the day before, when he had preached twice in the same day at Rose Green in Bristol, another public space. No fewer than twenty thousand people were present on this occasion! He wrote, "Surely God is with us of a truth. To behold such crowds stand about us in such an awful silence, and to hear the echo of their sing-

1. George Whitefield, *Journal of a Voyage from London to Savannah in Georgia* (London: Hunt and Clarke), 168.
2. Ibid.

ing run from one end of them to the other, is very solemn and surprising."[3]

Isn't that a vivid picture of his experience? Whitefield was describing something that frequently happens in crowds the size of which he was addressing. Because of the great distance between people in these large gatherings, when they sing together an echo develops. But Whitefield also speaks of the solemn silence too. He concludes, "I came home full of peace and joy in the Holy Ghost. What a mystery is the divine life! Oh, that all were partakers of it!"[4]

Whitefield records going to Bath on the next Monday, arriving at about 3 in the afternoon. He was weak and ill, and he had to lie down after dinner. But then he recalls:

> The hour being come for my preaching, I went, weak and languid as I was, depending on the divine strength, and, I think, scarce ever preached with greater power. There were about four or five thousand of high and low, rich and poor, to hear. As I went along [in the crowd], I observed many scoffers; and when I got upon the table to preach . . .[5]

Let us pause here to take in this scene, because it is amazing. Whitefield is standing on a table, without amplification, sick and weary, to preach to a crowd of about four or five thousand people. He continues:

> When I got upon the table to preach, many laughed; but before I had finished my prayer, all was hush and silent; and ere I had concluded my discourse, God, by his word, seemed to impress a great awe upon their minds; for all were

3. Ibid., 170.
4. Ibid., 170–71.
5. Ibid., 171.

deeply attentive, and seemed much affected with what had been spoken. Men may scoff for a little while; but there is something in this foolishness of preaching which will make the most stubborn heart to bend or break. "Is not my word like fire, saith the Lord, and like a hammer that breaketh the rock in pieces?" [Jeremiah 23:29][6]

Whitefield was a man of God who was raised up to preach the Word, and to preach it for the reviving of the church of God in Great Britain and also in this country.

Preaching and Revival Today

Has the time for preaching like Whitefield's passed? I suppose there might be some who would argue that it has, indeed, passed. There might be some who would argue that the Kingdom of God is now advanced by group Bible studies or the dissemination of Christian literature. There is a new perception of the life of the church conceived almost exclusively in terms of the equality of the body of Christ. It is sometimes even argued that one of the essential things for the development and spread of the Christian church is to draw the church away from a kind of clericalism—a centering on the preacher—and focus instead on the part that every Christian has to play. On this view, the focus on what every Christian is called to do is not only in how we witness to those who are outside the church, but also how those in the church are edified.

Surely everyone can agree that there is much that is thoroughly biblical in this newer emphasis. Every Christian is called of Jesus Christ. Every Christian has a calling. Every Christian has

6. Ibid.

an office to fulfill. We are all to give a reason for the hope that is in us. We are all to be ready to confess Christ's name before men. And we do minister to one another in the body of Christ. We are all given gifts, and those gifts are given to us so that we might be stewards of them. They were meant to be shared with one another, that we might labor for the upbuilding, reviving, and renewing of the church of Jesus Christ.

As an aside, we all know the importance of prayer in revival. The history of the church recounts many, many instances in which revival began in a particular place because of the prayer of some saint of God. This person may have had no gifts for preaching whatsoever, but simply prayed (often for many years) for the visitation of God's blessing on the church.

To return to our earlier point: it is true, of course, that much has been gained in recent years in understanding some of these biblical truths about the calling and the function of every believer in the work of Jesus Christ. But we must not let these newly realized truths (perhaps we can better call them old truths newly realized) hide from us the plain teaching of the Word of God. God teaches us that he makes use of the witness and the life not only of the individual believer, but also of those whom he raises up to be preachers of the gospel. Therefore, the place of preaching in the church of Jesus Christ as a means of revival is of utmost importance. It is still true that the preaching of the Word of God—the proclamation of the gospel of Jesus Christ—remains God's chosen means for stirring up the people of God, for building up the people of God, and for renewing the life of the people of God.

God has chosen the foolishness of preaching as the means by which he will show that the power is from him and not the fleshly imaginations of preachers. He does it this way to show that it is his work and not the work of man to renew his church.

And what I want to look at in this chapter is not only the fact that God has made preaching to be the chief means for the reviving and renewing of his church, but also something of the rationale for this as it is presented to us in the Word of God.

So we will look at three things: that revival by preaching is accomplished through God's chosen messengers, that it is accomplished through God's renewing message, and finally that it is for God's appointed purpose.

Revival Comes through God's Chosen Messengers

Preaching is the means for revival through God's chosen messengers. Those who preach the Word are called of God to preach, and they must not preach without God's calling. God's calling is indispensable to the preaching of the gospel. This much is true, of course, in the Old Testament as we read about the prophets that God raised up and commissioned. Jeremiah 23 is a magnificent chapter in this regard. A striking contrast is drawn between the false prophets and the true prophets.

There was no lack of preaching in Jeremiah's day. Indeed, there were plenty of prophets. And the prophets in those days, as is the case with some preachers today, were guilty of gross plagiarism. Verse 30 reads, "Therefore, behold, I am against the prophets, declares the Lord, who steal my words from one another." The problem in Jeremiah's day was this: if one prophet had a good thing going, another one picked up on it. So there was plenty of preaching; there was lots of it. But what was the matter with it?

God gives us the answer in verse 21: "I did not send the prophets, yet they ran; I did not speak to them, yet they prophesied." In other words, God has a problem with self-appointed prophets. Verse 32 continues, "Behold, I am against those who prophesy lying dreams, declares the LORD, and who tell them and lead my people astray by their lies and their recklessness, when I did not send them or charge them. So they do not profit this people at all, declares the LORD." The prophet or the preacher is not to be gauged by his eloquence or his pulpit drama. Some of these prophets were very vivid preachers; they had all sorts of dreams that they could describe. There were symbolic actions that they could perform. They had acts that they would put on with horns and whatever else.

There were, in short, all sorts of things that they could do to command a hearing. Moreover, they had a message that was immensely popular. The message was this: "Don't be afraid. Everything's going to be okay. You're the chosen people of God. Nothing can happen to the temple. Relax and know the wonder of God's blessing." They were the false prophets who said, "Peace, peace," when there was no peace. The main problem with it all, of course, was that these false prophets had not been sent by God in the first place.

The situation does not change in the New Testament. Prophets still had to be sent by God. In Romans 10:12–14, we see this principle applied to preachers:

> For there is no distinction between Jew and Greek; for the same Lord is Lord of all, bestowing his riches on all who call on him. For "everyone who calls on the name of the Lord will be saved." How then will they call on him in whom they have not believed? And how are they to believe in him of whom they have never heard? And how are they to hear without someone preaching?

Of course, some preachers would be very glad to stop right at this point, congratulating themselves on the indispensability of their position. But then notice the next verse: "And how are they to preach unless they are sent? As it is written, 'How beautiful are the feet of those who preach the good news!'" (Rom. 10:15, quoting Isa. 52:7). Prophets have to be sent of God. Preachers have to be sent of God. They must be called, chosen of God, and thrust forth by the Spirit of God into the work of the ministry of the Word.

Now, of course, the reverse of this is also true. That is, if God doesn't send them, they mustn't go. This corresponds to the truth that if God does send them, they must go. This much is clear from the combined witness of the Old and New Testaments alike.

The Preacher Must Be Called of God

The great fact that one must be called of God is illustrated in the very calling of the prophet Jeremiah. He condemned the false prophets who hadn't been sent, but we must remember that when he himself was sent, he was not very enthusiastic about it. In Jeremiah 1:5, God says to the prophet, "Before I formed you in the womb I knew you, and before you were born I consecrated you; I appointed you a prophet to the nations." In response, Jeremiah didn't say, "How much international celebrity will this mean for me?" After all, God had told him that he would be going to all the nations!

Now, of course, this was before the days of sermon downloads and other electronic means, so it wasn't evident to Jeremiah how he was going to have a ministry to all the nations. But listen to his reply: "Then I said, 'Ah, Lord GOD! Behold, I do not know how to speak, for I am only a youth'" (Jer. 1:6). At first glance, we might think that here is a wonderful answer. It was, in fact, better than other possible answers, but it was still not a satisfactory answer. It was acceptable for Jeremiah to be humble and realize that he was only a child. But listen to what God says next in response to Jeremiah (1:7–10):

> But the LORD said to me,
>
> "Do not say, 'I am only a youth';
> for to all to whom I send you, you shall go,
> and whatever I command you, you shall speak.
> Do not be afraid of them,
> for I am with you to deliver you,
>   declares the LORD."
>
> Then the LORD put out his hand and touched my mouth. And the LORD said to me,
>
> "Behold, I have put my words in your mouth.
> See, I have set you this day over nations and over kingdoms,
> to pluck up and to break down,
> to destroy and to overthrow,
> to build and to plant."

When God calls a man to the ministry of his Word as a prophet, that man must fulfill his ministry. This remains true in the New Testament as well, as we have already seen. Nevertheless, let us look at one more New Testament passage to make this abundantly clear.

In 1 Corinthians 9:16, Paul writes, "For if I preach the gospel, that gives me no ground for boasting. For necessity is laid upon me. Woe to me if I do not preach the gospel!" Now, the context in which Paul makes this statement is interesting. He is saying, "How can I really surprise the Lord? How can I do something for the Lord that he would not possibly expect?" Now, I know that sounds very un-Calvinistic, but it really is not. In effect, the apostle Paul is asking, "I love the Lord so much for what he's done for me—what can I possibly do to show the gratitude of my heart?"

So he answers his rhetorical question this way: "Well, I can preach." "But," he reasons, "if I preach, where is the gratitude in that?" He continues, "I'm called to preach. Woe is me if I don't preach. I must preach! What can I do in this predicament?" Then he says, "I've got it. I'm going to preach in Corinth without any salary, even though, as a minister of the Word, I've got a right to be supported by the Word. Nevertheless, there's a little something I can do: I'll just show them my love of the Lord by saying, 'I'll preach in Corinth without any salary at all.'"

The apostle's thinking here is brilliant, as he explains what motivates all his service for the Lord. But what he says about preaching is paramount. Essentially, he says, "I've got to preach because I've been called to preach. I have the gifts to preach, and I've got to use those gifts to preach." This is why in 2 Timothy 4:2, when he gives a charge to Timothy, he says, "Preach the word; be ready in season and out of season; reprove, rebuke, and exhort, with complete patience and teaching." Paul is saying to Timothy there, "This is your job. Fulfill your ministry. Do that which God has called you to do."

So those who are called to preach the Word are accountable to do it. To put it another way, those who are called to preach the Word are separated to the gospel. They are set apart to the proclamation and the explanation and the amplification of the Word of God. We saw as much in Jeremiah's call. God said to Jeremiah, "Before you were born I consecrated you" (Jer. 1:5). The apostle Paul knew that he had been separated to the gospel; in fact, he uses almost exactly the same language as the passage in Jeremiah: "He who had set me apart before I was born, and who called me by his grace, was pleased to reveal his Son to me, in order that I might preach him among the Gentiles" (Gal. 1:15–16).

This language of "separation" is made all the more interesting in the apostle's case when we remember that he was a Pharisee. The Pharisees' lives were centered around the fact that they were the separated ones, for that is what the very name *Pharisee* meant. So as a Pharisee, the apostle Paul was truly a "separated one"—set aside, set apart.

But after he met the risen Lord Jesus Christ, he had a new separation. He became a "Pharisee for the gospel," so to speak. He got a new sense of separation—not a separation to works of self-righteousness that he had come to deplore, but a separation now to the gospel of Christ that had been committed to him. So men of God are called to preach. They must preach to fulfill that calling, and they are separated to the work of preaching.

God Gifts Men for the Delivery of the Message

As we have seen, men are called by God to deliver his message—this is God's chosen method for reviving his church. Now we want to think about the fact that they are gifted of God to preach. When we use this language of "gifted of God," we mean that such men are gifted in the sense that they are those who have been brought to know the Lord Jesus Christ. They have the fruit of the Spirit and have a true and living faith in Christ; they love the Lord Jesus Christ.

But those called to preach the Word are given very special gifts for service. For example, Paul writes in Romans 12:3: "For by the grace given to me I say to everyone among you not to think of himself more highly than he ought to think, but to think with sober judgment, each according to the measure of faith that God has assigned." Now, a lot is packed into these words. Notice that the apostle Paul refers to "the measure of faith." He then proceeds to outline different gifts of faith that could be given, different gifts that could qualify people for different ministries.

The apostle Paul has begun this statement by referring to his own gifts: "By the grace given to me I say . . ." When Paul says that, it is the same thing as saying, "I say as an apostle." He is an apostle because he has the gifts of an apostle. And he exercises the gifts of an apostle. In an analogous way, those who have other gifts exercise their gifts and callings, so that when Paul lists these gifts, he includes the gift of ministering the Word of God (see v. 8).

Paul says something similar in 1 Corinthians 12:28: "And God has appointed in the church first apostles, second prophets, third teachers, then miracles, then gifts of healing, helping, administrating, and various kinds of tongues." He is saying that there are things to be done in the church for which we are qualified by special gifts that we have been given. As a kind of follow-up, Paul rhetorically asks in verse 29, "Are all apostles? Are all prophets? Are all teachers? Do all work miracles?" Of course, the answer to all those questions is "No." His point is that not all men are apostles, not all men are prophets, and not all men are teachers. We should also take note of the fact that there are foundational office-bearers, according to Paul, and then there are those who continue to serve the church through all its history. Among the latter group are the ministers of the Word—whether evangelists or pastors or teachers.

Let us look at still one more passage pertaining to Paul's apostolic ministry. It is a passage that is very illuminating for our understanding of what it means to have gifts such as those we have been discussing. In Ephesians 3:1–2, Paul writes:

> For this reason I, Paul, a prisoner for Christ Jesus on behalf of you Gentiles—assuming that you have heard of the stewardship of God's grace that was given to me for you.

Notice how beautifully he puts it! He doesn't say, "This gift has made me a prince of the church." He says, "This gift has made me a bondslave and a prisoner of Jesus Christ." Nevertheless, Paul sees the authority that is involved in the gift and the function that is involved. "I've received this gift, and it is a stewardship of the grace of God that is given me toward you. It makes me your servant. It enables me to serve you. I can serve you because I am a steward of the gift that God has given me," says the apostle Paul.

But how does he think about this fact in particular—that he has become a prisoner and a slave to those whom he serves? He answers in verse 4: "When you read this, you can perceive my insight into the mystery of Christ." So the apostle Paul is thinking here especially of that revelation given to him—which, in his case, was the special revelation of God. He was given to understand the meaning of the mystery of the gospel. So much so was this the case that he could refer to it as "my gospel," because he was the distinctive instrument raised up by God to receive the revelation of this mystery in its fullness.

So it is when God raises up preachers of the Word. He raises up men who have perception, who have understanding, who receive the mysteries given by apostolic revelation transmitted by the office of the apostles to the church of Jesus Christ, given to us in the Word of God. When I used to talk to a seminary student who was questioning his gifts, one of the things I liked to ask him was how the Bible was being opened to his understanding.

Sadly, there are men who can show up at seminary with the thought that perhaps they have been called to the gospel

143

ministry. And yet some may say, "You know, I don't get anything out of Bible study, really." Maybe that's shocking to you, but that happens sometimes. Some men, when you tell them something about the Bible, can write it down, but somehow they don't see it. It doesn't come alive for them. I don't want to try to speculate as to what the problems might be in individual cases. Of course, it's always possible that a man in seminary just has never come to a knowledge of Jesus Christ. It's also possible, however, that a man may be a true Christian, love the Lord, and yet not really have any deep giftedness in understanding the mysteries of the gospel of Christ. He's not the sort of person who is always seeing greater fullness, greater richness, and greater glory in the Word of God. It isn't true of him that every time he picks up this Bible he sees something there that he never saw before, that seems to open up with new fullness, new glory, and new power in the Scriptures.

Nevertheless, God gives gifts to men whom he calls for the ministry of the Word of God. And those gifts mean that a man who is called to understand Scripture has been given gifts to understand it and communicate it; he has been given gifts that involve a whole rich complex of things. In a sense, one cannot just "nail it down" with one or two characteristic traits. It involves a lot of things. It involves concern for people. It involves a burden for men's hearts. It is truly a rich gifting—and calling.

A man who is called to preach, therefore, is called as a chosen messenger of God. We must never forget the importance of God's calling in this whole process. God has not stopped calling men to preach the Word of God. God still does that, and God will still continue to do that until Jesus Christ comes again. As God does that, it is his purpose by that means to accomplish his own will in the church.

144

Revival Comes through God's Chosen Message

We have seen that there must be chosen messengers but that they must come with God's renewing message. And that means, in the first place, that the message must be *God-centered*. It is a message from God. The whole point of preaching is that it's God's Word that is proclaimed. In this sense, it is just the same today as it was with the prophets, even though preachers now do not receive a direct supernatural revelation from heaven as Jeremiah did. Yet preachers today proclaim the Word of God, which is his revelation from heaven.

Therefore, what the prophet said is still true. Jeremiah wrote,

> Let the prophet who has a dream tell the dream, but let him who has my word speak my word faithfully. What has straw in common with wheat? declares the LORD. Is not my word like fire, declares the LORD, and like a hammer that breaks the rock in pieces? (Jer. 23:28–29)

What is it that gives power to preaching? Well, according to Jeremiah, it's the message. It's the truth of the Word of God, and it's the fact that it is God who gives his Word. We see this continuing today. When the Word of God is faithfully preached, it has power—as Jeremiah put it, like a hammer that crushes rock.

If you want to see the fire of revival kindled, you must hear the preaching of the Word of God, not of the ideas of men. The problem with preaching today is that so much of it has strayed so far from the Word of God. When this happens, it is no longer the proclamation of the message that comes from God. This is because it is the Word of God alone that has power. In the Old Testament, the Word of God is associated with the breath of God, which, of course, is also the Spirit of God.

145

What, then, is the Word of God? It is his creating Word. God speaks and it is done. He commands and it stands fast. God breathes out his Word, doesn't he? What is a word? It is vocalized breath. Thus the Word of God is the vocalized breath of God. It is the very power of God to salvation to all who believe (see Rom. 1:17). And the preacher is called to preach the Word that comes from God, his inspired and inerrant Word.

We see this in spectacular fashion in the book of Acts again and again. We see references to the Word of God multiplying (cf. Acts 6:7; 12:24). Fascinatingly, we're not just told that the church spreads—we're told that the *Word* spreads. This is because the spread of the church is so totally dependent on the spread of the Word. The Word multiplies the church, if we can put it like that. The Word brings forth fruit because it is from God and has the power of God. This is what we see in times of revival.

This reminds me of an incident that happened years ago when I was at Westminster Seminary in Philadelphia. A student there came to see the dean because he was on the verge of leaving. What was his problem? "Well," he began, "your textbooks—some of them are so out of date." This man thought some of us professors needed a little encouragement to get more recent textbooks. He continued, "Well, I was a history major in college, and I just don't like the textbooks you have here." When pressed to say which textbook specifically, he answered, "It's a textbook that has stuff in it from back in the 1700s, and that stuff is so old and the language is so tough—well, I just don't like reading it at all." It turned out that the book in question was a history of the Great Awakening. The professor had assigned some primary sources to be studied, but this history major had no interest in primary sources—a fact alone that seems to indicate something about American education.

But if you were to actually read the book that this young man so disliked, it may have caused you to react in a similar fashion. There are sermons in that volume that would cause you to think, "How in the world could revival come from anything like this? This is just solid doctrine; that's all it is. Here's a sermon on justification by faith. Here's a sermon on the new birth. These are heavy doctrinal pieces. How could anybody get all excited from a sermon like that?" Of course we know the answer. It is the Word of God—that's why. It is the whole counsel of God. It's what God says. And that alone is what has the power.

The Word Is Focused on God

Of course, not only does it come from God, but it is also about God. It is the whole counsel of God that Paul preached to the Ephesian elders (see Acts 20:17–35). It's the great message of salvation that Paul details in Romans 11:36: "For from him and through him and to him are all things. To him be glory forever. Amen." Paul is not just talking about God's work in creation there. He is speaking primarily of God's work in salvation. That was his subject in chapters 9–11. The apostle concludes, "Salvation is all of God. It's all through him, and it's all unto him."

The word of God—God's message—is what a preacher ought to preach. If he preaches the Word of God, he preaches the message to the glory of God. He preaches that God's name might be praised. And Paul, in the book of Romans, tells us what the message is all about: it is the message of the righteousness of God. That's what the message is: the righteousness of God, revealed from heaven in Jesus Christ. It is also about the fact that this righteousness also reveals the wrath of God against sin.

But Paul goes on to say that there is a marvelous wonder about the gospel of grace, for it is the righteousness of God that

147

not only condemns sin, but also comes as the gift of God through Jesus Christ. The perfect righteousness of Christ is given to us and received by faith alone. Sin and salvation, creation and redemption, from the beginning to the end, the whole great story of the Word of God—it is all about God. It is God that must be preached. It is his glory that must be sought. This is doxological preaching—preaching that causes both preacher and congregation to burst forth in praise!

Oh, how little there is today of doxological preaching! Of preaching to the glory of God's name! How little there is of the kind of preaching like the apostle Paul's, dealing with the deepest and most difficult of theological themes! How does he end Romans 9–11? Does he end it by saying, "Well, I'm awful sorry, friends, that we ever got into this whole subject. I don't know how I ever got tangled in a thing like this. And I know what you're going to be asking me: how does this help me relate to my wife? And I didn't really mean to get so far afield from those things that really concern the problems of daily life"? Is that the attitude of the apostle Paul?

No.

He's looked at these mysteries, and what is his reaction as he preaches and teaches the church? His heart is filled with awe and wonder. It is lifted to God in praise. He cries out, "For from him and through him and to him are all things. To him be glory forever" (Rom. 11:36).

In both the Old Testament prophets and New Testament apostles, then, we find doxologies woven into their messages. This is what we need in preaching today. We need preaching that is filled with worship. Preaching that is not only before men but, more importantly, before God. Preaching that takes place before the face of the living God. Preaching that declares not only that the Word is from him, but that the Word is about him and the Word is unto him. Preaching that is praising God and calling others to join in that praise.

There is much to think about here in relationship to doxological preaching. The Old Testament is so full of the praise to God. The Psalms are singing the praises of God. Somehow praise has left our evangelism. We aren't calling people to join with us in the praise of the God of creation and the God of redemption, the One who is from the beginning and who is everlasting, and the One who has revealed to us the wonder of the depth of his mercy. Oh, the mercy of God! Oh, the height and depth of the mercy of God! Oh, the love of God, the holiness of God! The wonder of the Lord our God! Oh, how preaching for revival needs to be preaching about God! How we need to be again preaching the attributes of God, as God reveals himself in his Word to us!

The Word Is Focused on Christ

Preaching that is doxological and full of God's glory—preaching that is God-centered—is also going to be Christ-centered. It is going to be the preaching of Jesus Christ from all the Scriptures. The Old Testament, together with the New Testament, presents us with one central message: the message that God sent his only-begotten Son. And so the apostle Paul says, "I'm resolved to know nothing among you but Jesus Christ and him crucified" (see 1 Cor. 2:2). Paul was a specialist in his preaching. He specialized in Jesus Christ. He specialized in the heart of the gospel. He specialized in the Word of the cross. That Word of the cross, Paul tells us, is foolishness to the natural man. But Paul says to us that it is the power of God to salvation, to everyone who believes. God's "foolish wisdom" and God's "weak power" are what saves sinners. It pleases God by the foolishness of this message of the cross to save those who believe, Paul says.

149

Oh, what a threat it is to powerful preaching when preachers think they're too sophisticated to present the simplicity of the gospel! What awful things happen to preaching when it is too simple to present John 3:16, and to proclaim the love of God and the measure of God's love when he gave his only-begotten Son! Read the sermons from the time of the First Great Awakening by Jonathan Edwards, George Whitefield, and others. What you will find are the riches of Christ being set forth. And this is the kind of preaching that brings revival and renewal and change.

Revival Comes by the Word for God's Appointed Purpose

Finally, let us look at how revival comes through the preaching of God's Word for God's appointed purpose. What is God's purpose for our preaching? It is preaching that celebrates his triumph. In 2 Corinthians 2:14, Paul says, "But thanks be to God, who in Christ always leads us in triumphal procession, and through us spreads the fragrance of the knowledge of him everywhere." Jesus Christ leads us about in triumph. What Paul is talking about there is not his own triumph, but Christ's triumph. Christ has conquered. Paul is like a captive tied to the chariot of Jesus Christ. And he's being led about as a trophy of grace, as the number-one enemy general overcome by Jesus Christ and his mercy, now brought in the triumphal procession. It's almost as if our Lord says, "Here he is—Paul, my enemy—and now he's on display." And the apostle Paul says, "That's right. Here I am. I'm on display. I'm a bondslave of Jesus Christ." Notice how Paul concludes this section of 2 Corinthians:

For we are the aroma of Christ to God among those who are being saved and among those who are perishing, to one a fragrance from death to death, to the other a fragrance from life to life. Who is sufficient for these things? (2 Cor. 2:15–16)

All true preachers of the Word sympathize with that last phrase from Paul. The true preacher says with Paul, "Who is sufficient for these things?" How can a preacher do anything in his own strength, let alone preach? Some men have the experience of just being ready to preach and they just feel they can't do it, that they don't dare to attempt it. Surely in the power of the flesh one cannot. How can it depend on anything in the preacher when eternal issues are at stake—men's souls and men's eternal future? How can it depend on your presentation of the message? The preacher realizes that it cannot depend on him. It must be the power of God, the Word of God, and the work of God.

What a tremendous responsibility the preacher has! So Paul asks, "Who is sufficient for these things?" He asks this because, as he told the Corinthians, preaching is a savor not only of life unto life, but also of death unto death. When the keys to the kingdom of heaven are used, they are used to open the kingdom to those who receive the good news of the gospel by God's grace with gladness and those who turn aside to their own eternal ruin. Who is sufficient for these things? God's purpose is accomplished by true preaching—not only in those who are saved, but also in those who are lost.

But ministers are called primarily to be ministers of reconciliation. In that same epistle to the Corinthians, Paul does not say that we are called to be ministers of damnation; no, we are called to be ministers of reconciliation. We preachers plead with men to be reconciled to God (see 2 Cor. 5:17–21). And oh, what a ministry that is!

151

The Westminster Larger Catechism has a beautiful description of what happens when the Word is preached. Question 155 asks and answers: "How is the Word made effectual to salvation? The Spirit of God maketh the reading, but especially the preaching, of the Word an effectual means of enlightening." And then there's a proof text that goes with this question, which directs the reader to Nehemiah 8:8. This portion of Scripture recounts how the people of God, when they were brought back from exile, had the Word opened and the sense given to them. In other words, the preacher explained what it meant. So a preacher of the Word, if he's to be an enlightener, ought to tell you what the Bible is saying. He ought to explain it. This is a lost art in some circles. But that's what is involved: enlightening men's eyes so that they understand the truth of God.

Paul explains his calling like this in Acts 26:17–18: "I am sending you to open their eyes, so that they may turn from darkness to light and from the power of Satan to God." And when the law was found in the temple in the days of King Josiah, it was read, and they all mourned because they saw how they had broken the law of God (see 2 Kings 22:8–13).

We can summarize what preaching the law, in this case, is supposed to do in this beautiful clause: It is to "drive men out of themselves and draw them unto Christ." Driving and drawing. Of course, some preachers are better drivers than drawers, and some are better drawers than drivers, but the preaching of the gospel ought to do both. It drives men out of themselves so that they see that there is no hope in them. It reproves them, rebukes them, and lays upon them the guilt of sin.

Peter's preaching at Pentecost is a perfect example of this. His preaching drove men out of themselves; he accused them of their part in the death of Jesus Christ, and they cried out, "What shall we do?" (Acts 2:37). He drove them out of themselves, you see.

152

But then, gospel preaching draws men unto Christ. And in Acts 8:26–39, we read about Philip's drawing the Ethiopian eunuch to Christ, explaining from Isaiah 53 what it is that Jesus Christ has done. Gospel preaching goes on to describe not only the work in bringing sinners to Christ, but the continuing work of conforming them to his image, subduing them to his will, strengthening them against temptations and corruptions, building them up in grace, and establishing their hearts in holiness and comfort through faith, unto salvation, in the broadest sense. The whole fullness of God's perfect salvation in bringing us to Christ is expressed here: God is building us up so that we might know him, walk with him, and be conformed to his image.

This "driving and drawing" aspect of ministry was Paul's mission too. His great aim was to present every man perfect in Christ, and also to present the church as a pure virgin to Christ (see Col. 1:28; 2 Cor. 11:2). Individually and corporately, the apostle Paul wanted to see everybody brought to Jesus Christ and presented spotless before him. The Lord uses preaching to that end. He pours out the unction of his Holy Spirit upon the preacher, and he gives the renewing grace of the Holy Spirit upon the congregation.

I once had tea with Martyn Lloyd-Jones at his home in London, and in the course of the conversation I asked him a question. I said, "Dr. Lloyd-Jones, isn't it hard to tell sometimes whether you're preaching in the energy of the flesh or in the power of the Spirit?" And he looked at me, smiled, and said, "No, it's not hard." Well, I felt like I could crawl under the rug at that point! But he said, "When you're preaching in the energy of the flesh, you're going to feel exalted, you're going to feel lifted up. And when you're preaching in the power of the Holy Spirit, you're going to feel humbled, you're going to feel very low." He said, "When you preach in the power of the Spirit, your heart is going to be filled with awe at what it is that the Spirit of God does."

153

Well, I thought about what Lloyd-Jones said, and I prayed about it. I was on my way to give some messages in Austria. It was a very, very sleepy afternoon when I got there; the young people had been hiking, and I was speaking in a room that had a cozy fire but inadequate ventilation. It was very warm and comfortable—indeed, I was almost asleep before I got up to preach! And I figured I had to get through it somehow. And I looked at all these nodding heads, and I began to talk about the grace of God in Jesus Christ.

I recount this incident to reinforce exactly what Martyn Lloyd-Jones said. Because there was no power of the flesh that afternoon—I can assure you of that. The Spirit of God did choose to work. And there has never been a time in any of my pulpit ministry that I saw so evidently the power of God at work as that afternoon. When the message was concluded, it was time for everybody to go down to supper, yet nobody moved. They all sat there. Some were weeping and praying and dealing with the Lord personally. And I'm not used to handling that kind of thing, owing to my Presbyterian background! I was very uncomfortable, and so I went down to supper, and I was the only one down there.

But the Lord taught me something that day. He really did. He taught me to understand where the power of preaching comes from. And it's not the energy of the flesh. It's the power of the Spirit. It's the power of the Word of God.

Ezekiel's Example

We've got a good Calvinistic picture of men dead in trespasses and sins from the prophecy of Ezekiel, in the passage about the valley of the dry bones (Ezek. 37:1–10). And God says to the prophet, "Preach." So it is today. We preach the Word of God. And the Spirit of God moves. As Ezekiel saw in his vision, as it were, we see the bones brought together, covered with sinew and flesh. That's what God does. He does it through preaching. He did it of old, he continues to do it, and he will continue to do it.

Oh, pray! Pray for a renewal of the preaching of the Word of God in the power of the Holy Spirit! Pray for your pastor; pray for other men of God! Pray earnestly for them! For if we are to pray for renewal and revival in the church of Jesus Christ, we should pray for preaching that has power. We should pray for preaching that the Spirit of God uses for his purposes, to his glory.

ALLIANCE®

OF CONFESSING EVANGELICALS

What is the Alliance?

The Alliance of Confessing Evangelicals is a coalition of Christian leaders from various denominations (Baptist, Presbyterian, Reformed, Congregational, Anglican, and Lutheran) committed to promoting a modern reformation of North America's church in doctrine, worship, and life, according to Scripture. We seek to call the twenty-first-century church to a modern reformation through broadcasting, events, publishing, and distribution of Reformed resources.

The work centers on broadcasting, including such shows as *The Bible Study Hour* with James Boice and *Dr. Barnhouse & the Bible* with Donald Barnhouse. These broadcasts air daily and weekly throughout North America as well as online and via satellite.

Our events include the Philadelphia Conference on Reformed Theology, the oldest continuing national Reformed conference in North America, and many regional events, including theology and exposition conferences and pastors' events, such as reformation societies that continue to join the hearts and minds of church leaders in pursuit of reformation in the church.

The Alliance's online magazine is *reformation21*—a free "go-to" theological resource. We also publish the *God's*

Word Today online daily devotional, MatthewHenry.org, a source on biblical prayer, Alliance books from a list of diverse authors, and more.

The Alliance further seeks to encourage reformation in the church by offering a wide variety of CD and MP3 resources featuring Alliance broadcast speakers and many other nationally recognized pastors and theologians.